# A Young Man's Biblical Guide to Women, Sex, and Manliness

Josh LaGrange

Cover illustration by: Tom Gruenloh Jr.

Josh LaGrange is a pastor, church planter, husband, and father. He enjoys hunting, fishing, backpacking, camping, bow-making, kayaking, proclaiming the gospel, wrestling bears, and all other adventurous activities. (OK, not really the wrestling bears part).



ISBN: 978-1-934447-58-1



Printed by
Country Pines Printing
11013 Country Pines Road
Shoals, IN 47581
USA

To my wife.

*Many daughters have done nobly,*
*But you excel them all.*
Proverbs 31:29

# Table of Contents

# Note to Parents:

This book is meant for young men beginning their dating years. What I had in mind is a 16-year-old young man. I believe it's appropriate for young men as young as 12 and 13; however, here's my word of caution. My idea of what's appropriate at 13 may not be your idea of what's appropriate. I take a "full-disclosure" approach to parenting. In this book I talk about sex, certainly not graphically, but mentioning what the Bible teaches. If you're not ok with that, you probably shouldn't give this to him.

But let me caution you. If your child spends time around the world, then at 12 years old, he knows about sex. It gets talked about; he hears the jokes. He is getting the world's perspective. So often over-protective parents try to keep their children away from preaching and teaching about sex, but effectively what you've done is limit the child's knowledge. He or she receives years' worth of immoral education and absolutely no biblical education. I'm not talking about sex-ed in a classroom at school; I'm talking about what they hear in the locker room, the conversations on the bus home from football games. Your son is getting a worldly education. If you keep him from biblical teaching, you are ensuring that the *only* education he gets is worldly. Give him the Scriptures.

If you as a parent haven't read the Bible, you're in for a surprise. God's Word is graphic. He tells a man to enjoy his wife's breasts. He tells husbands and wives to be drunk on each other's love and exhilarated with their sex life. GOD SAID THOSE THINGS. Which means God thinks it's appropriate. If you have a different opinion, you're in disagreement with the God who created this world.

So give him this book, but much more importantly, put your family in the fellowship of a good (emphasis on "good") church. A church that teaches the Bible, preaches the gospel, and isn't afraid to say what needs to be said, even when it isn't popular. Put yourself and your son under that, and you will see what the Scripture means when it says, *"How can a young man keep his way pure? By keeping it according to Your word."*

# Introduction

I know you feel it, that burning, that craving, that aching for what is ultimate. God put that craving inside of you. You have desires in your soul for joy, real joy, big joy, satisfaction that is full. God put that inside of you because He wants that for you. There is a remedy for that desire; it's knowing God. Everyone feels it. That's why humans are running around trying every hobby, every drug, every drink, buying everything they can, trying everything they can because they're all trying to satisfy that craving in their soul. But there is only one place it's satisfied. It's in the God who created you, created joy, created sex, and created you with desires for these things.

God is a joy-giving God. God's desire for you is for you to be satisfied and full beyond what you could even handle right now. Understand—animals don't feel this. They don't crave meaning and purpose; they don't feel in their soul desires for what is ultimate. You do because God made you in His image. You want what's ultimate, and you need what's ultimate. You will know it in God through Christ. In Him you will taste of riches that resonate in your soul, that cry out that this is what you've been looking for. If you had nothing else in this world, but you had Christ, you would have everything.

But God has also given you other desires that are connected with this one. And for most of you, you feel the desire to love a woman and have her love you back. To be a man with brazen masculinity and protect her. To be a man of honor. To lead her. To conquer her enemies. For your wife to look at you with longing eyes. To have a love that sizzles. To have a marriage that displays the wisdom of God.

Well, I want to tell you—it's real. It exists. It's not just fairy tale myth. And guys—it's good. I mean—real good. But I also want to tell you it doesn't come naturally. At least, not anymore. It did for Adam and Eve, but this is a post-fall, cursed world. And the fact is, now, after the fall has brought ruin and chaos into this world, most marriages don't sizzle. At least not the right way.

The odds are you know of a lot of marriages that look miserable. It might even be in the home you're living in right now. You maybe see your parents merely tolerate each other. No spark. But you want something different. God has put within you soul-cravings; one of them is a desire for a marriage that is great.

Now, let me be clear; marriage isn't the singular purpose of life. Glorifying, knowing, loving, and enjoying God is. God's design is for some men and women to remain single like the apostle Paul, and for them God wants to use them to serve His kingdom in some ways that a married man can't. But for the majority of us, marriage is God's plan. It's the way we'll give Him glory with our lives. So let's be honest, for those who intend to get married, you want what's real. That's why He gave you these cravings. That's why you feel the craving for sex. God created you with that desire. Now slow down before you justify sin with that statement; sin has brought chaos into our bodies, and those good desires that God gave us get out of control, and our flesh wants to gratify ourselves immediately in perverse ways. We'll talk some more about that later, the flesh verses the Spirit, but for now know—God has put some of these basic desires in you. You've got to control them now that sin is in your body, but God created you with the desire for marriage and sex and love. So if you feel it, and you want to know how to treat a lady rightly, this book is going to help you. Not solve every issue, but help you.

But first you need to understand that if you want this, you're not going to get it following the examples of Hollywood or worldly wisdom. A recent event from a celebrity who attained goddess-like status shows this all too clearly.

A particular celebrity reached obscene popularity. Young men looked at her and drooled; young women wanted to be her, so they dressed like her, hung her posters on their wall, and signed up for her Twitters, so they could know everything that happened. And inevitably, they were taking life advice from her.

So when she was planning her wedding to her celebrity lover, it was all the craze. Middle-school girls were going to school and talking about her dress, day-dreaming about her "perfect" romance. She became a role model, but even more than that, an idol. The media elevated her to goddess-like status. She made millions of dollars in advertising leading up to it all. Then the day finally came. It was all the talk. That is, for 72 days anyway.

72 days was the length of her marriage. 72 days! After all of that hype, after all of that obsession, their marriage lasted less than a semester of college. Middle school girls wept. "But they looked so happy! (Sob, sob)." This is always the way sin promotes itself. It advertises. It paints a picture for you that makes it look amazing; it promises to give you everything, but it never delivers on lasting satis-

faction. It falls short every time. Satan wants you to think that he has the corner market on fun and happiness, and that God's ways are the ways of prudes and joy-less geezers, and He is on a giant campaign against fun and joy. And granted, you've seen some prudes and geezers, and a lot of times they promote their geezer-hood by quoting the Bible. But I'm here to tell you that that isn't God's ways.

In Proverbs 5:19 (NASB) God speaks to men about their wives. *"Let your fountain be blessed* [You know what He's talking about], *And rejoice in the wife of your youth. As a loving hind and a graceful doe, Let her breasts satisfy you at all times; Be exhilarated always with her love."* I know a lot of you are thinking, "That's in the Bible?" Yeah, that's in the Bible. Who do you think created sex?! God did. And He created it good, real good. The greatest sex that exists on this planet is that way because God made it that way. Satan is constantly trying to paint a picture of God that is boring. The reason he does that is because he knows the truth. In Song of Solomon God inspired Solomon to write a celebration of sex, romance, marriage, and love … and let me tell you—it's hot! They describe the passion that wells up in them, he describes her naked body, she says her hands drip with desire.

When I look my wife in the eyes and kiss her beautiful mouth, it's no cheap fling; she's mine and I'm hers. I cannot describe the exhilaration that that brings. It's an exhilaration that makes my knees weak, and you don't get that when sex is perverted.

When a teenage boy takes a girl's virginity in the back of a car, you don't get the soul connection that brings joy. When a man looks at pornography on his computer in the dark and touches himself, all that is, is dirty. And Satan can only offer a sex that is cheaper than the real thing.

So my point after all that is this. If you want what's real, what's ultimate—you go to the One who created it. God has spoken. The God who created man and woman, the God who created marriage, and sex, and love has spoken. If you want worldly wisdom then put down this book and go follow your temporary Hollywood idols on Twitter. By the time this book is published they ought to be on their fourth or fifth marriage by now. But if you want God's ways, keep reading.

# 1

# Understanding the Fairer Sex

Girls are crazy. The end.

(If you would like to learn how to deal with the crazy, please continue).

I don't think I'll ever forget it. Equality was big in our culture at the time, and even though I was a Christian, I didn't know it, but culture had influenced me. We pulled up to a gas station to fill up before our date. I looked at her and told her it was her turn to pump. So she got out and filled up the tank as I sat there in the car like a bum. A young man at the next pump looked over at us kind of puzzled and said to my girlfriend, "Ain't no reason you should be pumping gas with a MAN sitting in that front seat." It infuriated me; I wanted to get out of that car and get in his face. But just as quickly as the anger came, a wave of shame swept over my body. I wasn't a man. That was the move of a wuss. I wish there had been a book like this when I was a teenager. I wish someone had told me, "This is how a godly man treats a lady, and anything else is just shameful." But I didn't have this book, so I made a lot of dumb mistakes.

See, God has created ladies uniquely. And because of their uniqueness, God calls her husband to care for her in a special way. God says in Jeremiah 1:5, *"Before I formed you in the womb I knew you."* In Psalm 139:14 the author, through the inspiration of the Holy Spirit says, *"I will give thanks to You, for I am fearfully and wonderfully made, And my soul knows it well. My frame was not hidden from You, When I was made in secret, And skillfully wrought in the depths of the earth."* Genesis 1:26-27 says, *"Then God said, 'Let Us make man in Our image, according to Our likeness'... God created man in His own image, in the image of God He created him; male and female He created them."* God specifically created woman different from man.

I know that you're thinking right now, 'Duh.' But it's not 'duh.' You're living in a culture that is dominated by feminism and political correctness, and it's trying to tell you that the only difference is body parts. But that ridiculous belief defies all logic. God has created you different from her. God created her with a delicate blend of emotions, hormones, chromosomes, and DNA to make her female. The difference is more than parts.

But it's this confusion over "equality" that is causing so much chaos for young men, but especially for young women. The culture keeps trying to convince everyone that women should act just like men. (Hence my belief that it was her turn to pump gas). But God didn't create you the same. Both men and women have equal WORTH before God, but they're not the same. God didn't create her to bear the burden of great weight on her back, and go to war, and deal with conflict like He did you. God gave her a smaller frame, with smaller muscles, and a different emotional make-up specifically for her task. Just the same that God didn't create you with the ability to nurture like she can. I can't even come close to multi-tasking the way my wife can. If I have to watch kids and cook supper at the same time, something's not making it through that experience. Can some women lift heavy weights and fight in war? Yes. And can some men nurture and multi-task? Absolutely. But to deny there is a difference because of exceptions is to deny logic that is smacking you in the face. YOU'RE DIFFERENT!

And God made you different to fulfill different roles. Men, God created you to take care of a woman. God made her delicate. 1 Peter 3:7 says, *"You husbands in the same way, live with your wives in an understanding way, as with someone weaker, since she is a woman; and show her honor as a fellow heir of the grace of life, so that your prayers will not be hindered."* You can see why our feminist culture hates the Bible. God has the audacity to call women "weaker." But for crying out loud, she is weaker! Every time someone denies that, they're denying the obvious! There's a reason the girl's basketball team doesn't play the boy's team, they'd get demolished! There's a reason most schools (none that I know of) have a girl's tackle football team. They are weaker. That doesn't make them inferior, and that doesn't make their worth diminish. It means they were created different. With fine china, its delicateness makes it have value. You treat that china differently than you other items. That's the sense in which God speaks to us men. Treat her like fine china. She is more delicate, so that means you use more caution, patience, and understanding. Isn't it amazing that Scripture's truth is so plainly clear? No matter how much the culture tries to deny it, the truth is right there every time men and women play sports on different teams.

God has called you to treat a girl with gentleness because of the way she's wired up. Often times we're tempted to get frustrated with ladies because of their emotions, or the way they can sometimes fret over things that we don't think matter. But this is part of the beautiful package. And God calls you to be a man of honor and strength to show grace, and patience, and understanding, and sympathy to love her.

So after that hear this—God expects you to treat a woman like a treasure. Listen to Ephesians 5:28-29. *"So husbands ought also to love their own wives as their own bodies. He who loves his own wife loves himself; for no one ever hated his own flesh, but nourishes and cherishes it, just as Christ also does the church."* How are you to treat a woman? Several things we're told there, but notice the phrase that God uses, you are to nourish and cherish her. Cherish. She is to be precious to you like a treasure.

You all know that men have claimed the Bible as their basis for treating women like slaves, bossing them around from the couch, yelling for another bag of chips. But that's not a man, that's an ape. And it's not biblical. God does call you to be the head, the leader (we'll talk more about that later), but the way you lead, is by sacrificing. You lead the way in service. Jesus led the apostles by washing their feet. As a man you're the one to take the hit; you step in front of the difficulties; you're the first to pick up the yoke, and you carry the bulk of the weight. That's how you lead, not like an ape yelling for another Twinky. Be a man, treat her like she's precious.

You are to respect her. God created her wonderfully. She's intricate and complicated, but she's made in the image of God. God, on purpose, made her weaker than you. Take honor in your calling to be her protector. That's what those muscles are for, not flexing in the mirror.

# 2

# Stand Up and Be a Man

Be a man, not a sissy. In 1 Corinthians 16:3 Paul writes, *"Be on the alert, stand firm in the faith, act like men, be strong."* God—wants you—to be a MAN. Unfortunately there are a lot of males with a Y-chromosome and "parts" who aren't MEN. They've never put away their childish things. They're still walking around like toddlers believing that all the world ought to be serving them, and when it doesn't happen they throw their little temper tantrums, and when his wife or girlfriend won't give him what he wants, he pouts. That's not manliness, that's shameful.

God has a lot to say on manliness. God created men—real men. Look at 1 Chronicles 11:10-47 and look at what some of these men did. (Well go on, read it).

Did you catch the part with Eleazar? Everyone was running away from a band of Philistines, and Eleazar just stops in the middle of a field, turns around and faces the band by himself. He was tired of running; he met them head-on in battle and delivered a divine smack-down on those soldiers. Then there's Benaiah. We're not told a lot about him, but one day there was a lion caught in a pit on a snowy day. So what's the obvious thing to do when you see a lion in a pit on a snowy day? Why, jump down into the pit with the lion, that's what. Benaiah jumps down in there with him. Why? We're not told, but my assumption is the man was high on testosterone. And in the pit he killed the lion. These are men! Real men. Not v-neck wearing, skinny-jeans models, these were men. God made them real men, and they're praised in Scripture for being masculine mighty men.

When a man acts like a woman it's called being "effeminate." And it's not ok with God. God didn't create men to act like women. In fact in the Old Testament there's a verse that says if a man dresses like a woman he was to be stoned. God's not down with men getting in touch with their feminine side. You don't have a feminine side; you're a man, through and through. If you happen to be a young man who struggles with some of that, realize that God is gracious and there is hope. With His help you can overcome those tendencies, just like we can overcome any fleshly tendency by the work of the Spirit. So take hope, but you also need to realize that it's not ok, no matter what Oprah says. You're called to be a man. So put down the high-heels and start acting like a man. But don't get the wrong idea. Our culture sometimes thinks that a man is someone who spits, cusses, sleeps with lots of women, and likes to drink. But that's not God's definition of a masculine man. David was a masculine man. David grabbed a lion by the beard and killed it. But David wasn't a tobacco spitting ape. What made David great was his godly masculinity. Let me give you a little summarization of what that means.

# 1) Real Men Take Responsibility

Responsibility is rising up to do what needs to be done and not waiting for someone else. In Genesis chapters one through three we see God create the world, as well as a special garden, and He gave it to the man to take care of. Eve helped and worked as well, but it was the man's responsibility to see that it happened. God has given men work to do. You are to do something with your life. That doesn't have to be anything that makes you famous or what the world considers successful, but you are to work.

In Scripture we're told about some men who never achieved earthly greatness, but they rose up and they tilled the ground to provide for their family, and that's honorable. Men do what needs to be done. Children cry for others to do it. If you spend any time in leadership you will notice very few people are willing to step forward and take on all the responsibilities for a project. Some aren't willing to work at all; others are willing to work but unwilling to bear the burden of the responsibility. It's risky, you get blamed, it's more work, but part of being a man is being willing to carry that load.

As a husband and father, you will have the tremendous responsibility to care for a wife and a family, to lead them, and provide for them. That's why a lot of men walk out on their families; they are selfish and want to live for themselves. This is why a lot of men are choosing not to marry and live in their mommy's basement. They want to play video games and goof around and don't want the burden of being responsible. Which is better than walking out on a family, but it's still a waste! This is what God made you for. This is what men do. They rise up and do what needs to be done. Children pass off responsibility, men rise up and meet it head on. So if you don't want to care for a wife and have responsibility, by all means, keep living in Mommy's basement and playing your video games, but the real men of the world are going to be doing something with their lives. Real men step up to the plate and take responsibility.

## 2) Real Men Lead

Ephesians 5:22 - 6:4 is one of the clearest passages in the Bible where God lays out the order of the family and gives each person his or her calling. It's a jam-packed section, so we will refer to it numerous times in this study, and here is one of the truths that comes out. In 5:22 God says, *"Wives, be subject to your own husbands, as to the Lord. For the husband is the head of the wife, as Christ also is the head of the church, He Himself being the Savior of the body."*

We're also told in the New Testament that the leadership of the church is to be comprised of men. 1 Timothy 2:12 says, *"But I do not allow a woman to teach or exercise authority over a man."* He's speaking in regard to the teaching ministry of the church. What that means is, God has called men to lead. Every husband is a leader; every father is a leader. It doesn't matter whether he wants to be or not, he is. Whether he leads his family well or not, he IS the leader. Statistics from our culture show this. Nearly 9 out of 10 runaway children come from homes where there is no father. 90%! 6 out of 10 of all youth suicides come from homes where the father either isn't around, or isn't involved. Girls are many times more likely to have eating disorders and be sexually active when her father is not around or uninvolved. Prisoners, drug users, and rapists all have this in common, the overwhelming majority of them had no father around or had an uninvolved father. Do you see what that's saying? Even when a father isn't around, he still determines the spiritual direction of his family! And here is one that is incredibly enlightening. A child is 20 times more likely to continue attending church if his father is active in his spiritual upbringing. 20 times more likely![1]

If you're going to be a husband, then you WILL be a leader. You WILL be the head of your wife and the authority over your children. What you're called to do is live that. Leading is about being active, not passive. Sitting on the sidelines hoping not to be seen is not what God made you to be. There is a broken world that needs ministering to. There is an endless amount of work that could be done. The church needs godly men to jump in and say, "Let's do this."

Picture your future family in a vehicle (I know you don't want to picture a minivan, so picture a full-size truck with an extended cab for your 12 kids in the back). As you're driving through life, who's in the driver's seat? God says you are. Whether you want to be or not, you're in the seat. You are going to determine where your family is headed. In many families the dad is asleep at the wheel and his wife has had to crawl over and grab the wheel. She's leading the family; she's bringing them to church (thank the Lord); she's building the children's character; she's making the decisions about the direction of the family—all because dad's asleep at the wheel. God hasn't called your wife to that role, he's called you. And thank God for the wives who have reached over and grabbed the wheel to lead their families because somebody's got to do it. But if you leave your wife in that position you're shirking your responsibilities. It's your job to lead. Which means, you're going to have to figure out how to do it. It doesn't matter if it's awkward to you; it doesn't matter if you don't feel like you know how; you've got to figure it out.

Passivity is your enemy. Being passive is seeing problems and then ignoring them. Letting it go, hoping it will go away. It's procrastinating, saying, "I'll get to it eventually." Responsible leadership is about rising up and dealing with problems and work head on. In your family, in the church, in society—godly men lead.

## 3) Real Men Protect

Let's look at more from the Ephesians 5 passage. Verse 25 says, *"Husbands, love your wives, just as Christ also loved the church and gave Himself up for her."* A lot of times when people read this passage they think it to be unfair. Wives are called to be subject to their husbands and respect their husbands, but the primary command given to husbands is to love their wives. That seems a lot easier than the command given to wives; it seems like husbands get the better deal. That is, until you consider how we're supposed to love our wives—*as Christ also loved the church and gave Himself up for her.* You are to love your wife in the same way, in the same manner, and with the same sacrificing tenacity with which Christ has loved the church.

There are a multitude of ramifications from that, but one of them is—you are to lay your life down for your bride. There are two primary ways you are to do that. Number one, husbands are called to be willing to die in a moment's notice to save their wives and their children. If a man with a knife jumped you on the street, you tell her to run while you hold him off. If you're hiking, and a bear bursts onto the trail and charges you, you take the bear. You get the picture, in any scenario of danger, you face the danger while you do everything possible to protect. We've got to be willing to do that in an instant with no hesitation. It can't just be a decision we make when the bear bursts onto the trail; it's got to be a mindset you keep at all times. You are her protector; that's your identity, take it seriously. Make the decision ahead of time to act with courage if a moment arises when it's necessary.

The second aspect of laying down your life is this—you are to die daily for her blessing. This is the language Scripture uses to talk about saying "no" to our flesh and putting others first—dying. Paul said, *"I die daily."* What he meant was, he's obeying Christ's command in Luke 9:23—*"If anyone wishes to come after Me, he must deny himself, and take up his cross daily and follow Me."* The call is to resist those cravings you feel in your flesh to serve yourself and indulge your lusts. God calls you to imitate Christ in sacrificing yourself for the good of your bride. That means every single day dozens of times throughout your day choosing to serve her. That means getting up and going to work; that means thinking about how to encourage her; that means sending her a text that says, "I love you," because you know it would touch her heart; it means doing the dishes once in a while because it brightens her day; it means 1,000 small ways you intentionally do something or say something to bless her rather than sitting there like a lump on a log (which is easy). It means exerting mental energy thinking about how to bless her and exerting physical energy serving her. Jesus washed the disciples' feet. That's not normally what leaders do. But Christ was showing us something different. He was showing us the way of leadership in the kingdom of God. As a husband you will have hundreds of opportunities a day to do the same kind of thing. That's dying daily.

Additionally, men are called to protect more than just our wives and children. We are to protect all innocent life. God calls us to protect the widow and the orphan. You've no doubt heard the quote, "The only thing necessary for evil to prevail is for good men to do nothing." God has called men to meet evil with justice and bravery, not passivity and indifference. So far as you are able, do not allow others to be mistreated. Develop that mindset and be that man with your girlfriend or wife and the rest of society. Don't wait for someone else to come along, rise up and protect. One of the worst things you've learned in school is that there's never a time for violence, but the fact is, there is. It's necessary. There's a time to fight; there's a time to go to war, and there's a time to kill. Not for selfish reasons, but for the protection of innocent life you had better believe that God has called you to rise up and do it.

So considering all of those things, do you see just how disgusting it is for a man to hurt a woman? That's not manliness, that's childishness. Manliness is protecting others. Manliness is saying as the ship is going down, "Women and children first into the lifeboats!" That's real manliness. A real man takes a hit rather than allowing a woman to be harmed. A real man sacrifices so that others are protected. Real men serve their country by walking into war zones to meet evil head on, so that others will be spared of it. A male who treats his wife like she's his doormat-servant isn't a real godly man. A male who sits in a recliner and barks orders at his wife to get him another bag of chips, that's not manliness. Real men protect.

## 4) Real Men Are Honorable

Honor is esteem, respect, or glory. Real men are the kind of men whom others look on with a sense of respect. Their character demands esteem. They are esteemed highly because their conduct and their character displays greatness and integrity. Character is who you are in the depths of your heart meshed together with the convictions you hold. A man of honorable character would take a beating rather than lie. A man of honorable character would take a kick in the teeth rather than act disgracefully. Loyalty, integrity, bravery, goodness—that's what this is about. God wants honorable men.

So consider this, there is absolutely nothing honorable in a man leaving his family. That's what children do, walk away when things are tough. Real men see the linebacker coming through the line, grit their teeth and the meet him head-on. Yeah it hurts, but that's why God gave you what He's given you. It is the opposite of manliness for a husband to leave his wife. It is the opposite of manliness for a man to cheat on his wife. It is the opposite of manliness not to work, not to provide. There's nothing about that which is honorable!

I hope you can start to see that real masculinity is very different from the picture that is painted of masculinity in our culture. On one hand you have the picture of masculinity that looks very feminine, we've already seen that to be dishonorable. But on the other hand, there is this image of masculinity that sees men as foul-mouthed, perverted, sin-loving, pagans who sit around drinking beer and looking at porn. All of that is not honorable and therefore not masculine! That's shameful. Nothing about that draws esteem for honorable character. That's Satan's version of masculinity. Satan's version is a selfish man who fathers children with numerous different women and then weasels out of paying child support. Satan's version of masculinity is a player who sleeps with as many women as possible. It's shameful and the men who image it forth ought to be embarrassed! God created real men! You will know the most joy in your life when you be what God's called you to be!

## 5) Real Men Are Disciplined

Part of strength is learning to make yourself do what is good and refrain from that which is harmful and wicked. If you play football, then you know that it is not easy to wake up after 4 days of two-a-day practices and get out of bed and go to the field. You're lying there in bed and your body aches more than you thought was humanly possible and the thought crosses your mind, "I could just say I'm sick." But inside of you there's a conviction that makes yourself get up and do what you've committed to do. That's discipline. It is learning to make yourself do certain things and refrain from others for the good of your body and your character. It's discipline that forces you to stop eating when you know you've had enough, but your flesh wants more. It's discipline that sets aside time to read your Bible when your flesh really isn't feeling in the mood. Discipline is what molds you to be great.

In 1 Timothy 4:7 the Holy Spirit commands you, *"Discipline yourself for the purpose of godliness."* That involves disciplining every part of who you are: your body, your mind, your heart, your soul. It means watching over your thoughts, your eyes, your hands, all of you. Discipline yourself to rise out of bed at a certain time to guard against laziness. Discipline the amount of food you allow yourself to eat. Discipline the amount of TV you watch, so your mind doesn't turn to mush. Discipline yourself to finish your homework. Discipline yourself to read your Bible, spend significant time in prayer each day, and memorize Scripture.

It's about learning how to say "no" to the flesh. That's part of what it means to be human. Animals merely follow their impulses. It's interesting that a lot of what God commands us in Scripture is about living like you are made in the image of God, as compared to the animals. When you lose the ability to say "no" you're acting like an animal. Old theologians used to call the lusts of the flesh the "animalistic desires." So hear the call in this—act like men, not like apes.

As a young man this has a world of ramifications. If you will begin now to discipline your time, you will be so glad you did later on in life. The way you get buff is not by lifting hard at the gym one day, or even one month. It doesn't come quickly; it's a long slow process. But if you commit yourself to the slow steady work of it, you will see the results. And much more importantly, if you will begin now to seek God, to do simple things like reading and memorizing Scripture, IT WILL CHANGE YOUR LIFE! You will have more joy if you discipline yourself to begin now, however old you are.

Give yourself to the simple things that everyone can do, and everyone should do, but not every one does. For some things, even five minutes a day can change your life. Five minutes a day of an ab workout will yield incredible results. And as a man there is even spiritual value in working your body. Don't get obsessed with it, that's just vanity, but as a man God gave you a body capable of strength, and you should try to reach your potential. But infinitely more important is that you discipline yourself for obedience, and worship, and seeking God. If you devoted five minutes a day to memorizing Scripture, in a year you could memorize the entire book of James! That's just five minutes a day!

Discipline yourself to do certain actions. Those actions then turn into habits. And habits done over the long haul, with the right heart, produce character. And character is what we're after.

## 6) Real Men Love

David was a man's man. He is described in the Bible as a muscular good looking guy. He is a guy who literally did hand to hand combat with bears and lions. That's a man! David took responsibility, David led, David lived honor, and David also knew how to love. Look what David says to God in Psalm 63, *"My soul thirsts for You, My flesh yearns for You, In a dry and weary land where there is no water."*

Listen, David wasn't in touch with his feminine side. If you're a man you don't have a stupid feminine side! When David expressed deep emotion from his heart and wrote poetry, it wasn't acting feminine, it's altogether masculine. As a man God made you with a heart, a soul, an inner man, and emotions. Those emotions are to be different than a woman's, but they are still emotions.

Solomon was another man's man and look how he speaks to his wife. *"You have made my heart beat faster, my sister, my bride; You have made my heart beat faster with a single glance of your eyes, With a single strand of your necklace. How beautiful is your love, my sister, my bride! How much better is your love than wine, And the fragrance of your oils Than all kinds of spices! Your lips, my bride, drip honey; Honey and milk are under your tongue."* Here's the point, it is altogether masculine to express love and beauty to the woman you love. When Solomon spoke those words to his bride, she melted.

It's not manly to be unable to feel and unable to express beauty to the woman you love. That's acting like an animal. It's not human, it's dog-like. A man who feels no affection, expresses no affection, speaks no words of love to a woman, but then wants sex from her, that's not a man, that's an ape. A man who can't express love to his children, that's unmanly, that's monkey-like.

As a man of God you need to have strength. You need to be able to step in front of a bus without hesitation to save a life. That's manliness. But it is also manliness to feel deeply, for your soul to be stirred, to have strong affections. Sin diminishes that ability. The more godly you become the more affections you will have, towards God and others. So as a man, feel deeply, then, learn to express that to the woman you love.

## 7) Real Men Are Courageous

Implied in every part of what we have seen above, is that courage is required. It takes courage to step up and lead. It takes courage to put yourself out there, take on a project, be the point man that people look to. What oftentimes keeps men from leading when they are needed is cowardice. What keeps a dad from disciplining his four year old in Wal-mart when she's throwing a fit is fear. God calls men to have a spine. Ambrose Redmoon said, "Courage is not the absence of fear, but rather the judgment that something else is more important than fear."

Courageous men are not testosterone crazed freaks who feel no panic, but men who find a way to rise above it. The soldier looking out at a battlefield of bullets flying and people dying finds a way to harness his emotions and step up. The body wants to lock up, or cower in the corner and hope not to be seen, but the courageous men want to be the ones to accomplish the goals. Fearful husbands passively sit back and let their wives walk into sin and foolishness because they fear the conversation of warning them. Courageous men see the bigger issues, see the danger, and take the risk.

Leading is always risky. That's why fools rush into it unprepared, and cowards refuse to have any part of it. You WILL be made to look like a fool at times, that's part of it. But have zeal for God, and the sense of calling that steps up and does it anyway. Theodore Roosevelt said this:

> It is not the critic who counts; nor the one who points out how the strong person stumbled, or where the doer of a deed could have done better. The credit belongs to

> the person who is actually in the arena; whose face is marred by dust and sweat and blood, who strives valiantly; who errs and comes short again and again, because there is no effort without error and shortcoming; who does actually strive to do deeds; who knows the great enthusiasms, the great devotion, spends oneself in a worthy cause; who at the best knows in the end the triumph of high achievement; and who at worst, if he or she fails, at least fails while daring greatly. Far better it is to dare mighty things, to win glorious triumphs even though checkered by failure, than to rank with those timid spirits who neither enjoy nor suffer much because they live in the gray twilight that knows neither victory nor defeat.

YEAH! Does that not make you want to risk? I'm not talking gambling with the stock market, but do you not want to try great things, dare adventures, be a man, step out there and do what is hard while others sit back afraid?!

We have the greatest adventure in the history of the cosmos, the kingdom of God! God has swept you up into the original epic, the adventure that starts and ends all other adventures. There are unreached people in the Amazon rain forest who have never heard the name of Jesus Christ, let alone been given the opportunity to repent and believe. Jesus isn't coming back until all the nations have heard the message of the gospel and souls are saved from every tribe, tongue, people, and nation. Will you tell them?! Adventures like that are just screaming for a man to go make it happen!

In the history of the church, over and over, it's been men with an adventurous spirit, willing to go sleep on a jungle floor who have made that stuff happen. There is a godly outlet for those manly desires. God wants to use your courage, your sense of adventure, your toughness, and yes, even your camping skills.

Your church needs men! So many churches are full of women who will lead and husbands who are lazy. God's calling you to courageously be willing to get stepped on, get your face marred, be misunderstood, but along the way see some fruit. Don't be afraid to fail. Prepare wisely, but attempt great things. Go ahead and fail. At least you've done something, while the slobs sit on their couches always telling themselves, "I could do better … if I wanted to."

Be courageous. Lead. Take risks. Get laughed at. Die. Be forgotten. But live a life that has meaning.

## 8) Real Men Stand Strong in the Faith

*"Be on the alert, stand firm in the faith, ACT LIKE MEN, be strong"* (1 Cor 16:3). Do you notice how every part of that verse is manly? Alert like a soldier standing guard, putting a line in the sand that says, "This far, and no farther." Standing firm like a protector who is watching over the innocent. Wolves are circling, the cowards have all run away, but the Man stands there in the middle, determined, "I will not be moved." And, *be strong*. God created men to be strong. That attribute is to define you. It needs to define you physically. Seriously. You will not fulfill God's will for your life by being a sissy. You don't need to oil up and flex in a mirror, but barring health make-ups you cannot help, you need to be strong so you can be a protec-

tor and worker. But that's not what God is speaking of in this verse of Scripture.

This verse calls us men to be strong IN THE FAITH. Meaning, not children in the faith, not weak in the faith, not spiritual pansies, but mature in the faith. It is a lie that has been spread by the enemy of God, but it has taken root. Many men believe it is feminine to be godly, when the fact is, it is altogether manly. The truest definition of what it means to be manly, came from God. And you have no doubt seen bad examples of effeminate men who are so soft spoken they couldn't lead on a battle field, champion their weakness as "religious." But don't let that cloud your eyes from seeing the real manliness that God wants you to become. Manliness means being godly. Think about every good attribute of a real man, and every part of it is godly. Courage, leadership, honor, conviction, etc. The opposite of each of these is an evil vice. Cowardice, passivity, being a sleeze-bucket who just looks out for himself. Genuine masculinity is godly masculinity, and sitting under the preaching, teaching, and instruction of God's Word is what brings this about in you.

In Hebrews 5:12 we read this, *"For though by this time you ought to be teachers, you have need again for someone to teach you the elementary principles of the oracles of God, and you have come to need milk and not solid food."* The author of Hebrews is telling the believers he is writing to that they have not been faithful to study, to learn, to meditate, and to be in the Word. There is the expectation that every Christian immerse himself in the Word of God and develop a robust faith and a working knowledge of the Bible, but these believers had been lazy. God expects you to grow, to study, to regularly meditate on the Scriptures, all of which transforms you.

You want to be a great man? You need to be transformed from the inside out. It's God's Word that does that work. The preaching you get in worship, the teaching you get in Sunday School and small groups, the instruction you get in good books, and the renewing that takes place when you study the Bible for yourself, all of that is God's method of growing you. So God wants you to know the Bible; He expects you to study theology; He commands you to be a regular reader of the Bible, and then to apply it, to be a doer of the Word and not merely a hearer.

The church has a major problem trying to get men to step up and do something. So many men will lead at their job, come home and coach their boy's baseball team, but we can't get them to take up offering in the church service. That comes from not seeing what really matters, that life is about God, not about their money, their job, and their hobbies. The summation of your life is how you live unto God, for His glory. And the root of that misunderstanding is weakness in the faith. Set your sights on becoming a godly man; then stand there, and don't let anything move you off that course.

## 9) Real Men Fulfill Their Purpose

We don't have to go far into the Bible before God tells us what it's all about, what our purpose is, why we were created, and how we can live so that our life has meaning. In fact, if you start at the beginning, you won't make it out of the first chapter of the Bible, Genesis 1, before God smacks you in the face with it. *"In the beginning—GOD."*

It's all about Him, He is the starting point, center point, and end goal. All things are *"from Him, through Him, and to Him." "He is before all things and in Him all things hold together."* God is not a side item. Your life is not about sports, a job, a woman, a family, and oh yeah, everybody needs a little Jesus in their life. Jesus is the climax of all of history, what this world was about before it was even created. He will bring this world to its consummation, and all of eternity will be about God and His glory. That's the program, you need to get with it.

When God created man, He created us in His own image. That's not just information, that's your purpose. You were created to be a mirror. A mirror that reflects back the glory of God. He is great, and wonderful, and glorious. He made you in ways that are like Him and He calls you to live and have character that is like His —holy, loving, gracious, zealous for what is good, etc., and when you do, the world sees God's wonderfulness in you. All things were created to show God's awesomeness, including you. The purpose and meaning of your life—is God. He created you for Himself. The sooner you come to grips with that the happier you will be. So long as you think you exist to rule yourself, the more offended you will be when all the world doesn't bow down to you. You exist for God. You belong to Him. The meaning that you're looking for is found in Him.

1 Corinthians 10:31 says, *Whether then you eat, or drink, or whatsoever you do, do all to the glory of God!* God wants you to sleep for His glory; God wants you to eat breakfast for His glory; God wants your work to be about His glory, He wants the way you do your family to be for His glory. He wants you to love Him so supremely that you

gladly submit to His rule, and it is your delight to live to obey Him, and your entire life becomes worship to God—intentional worship to Him. And all of that serves to magnify His name, to reflect His glory, you become what God created you to be. And that's why you breathe!

A cup serves one purpose, to hold liquid. That's what it was created for. If a cup does not hold water, what do you do with it? You throw it in the trash because it is useless. Useless is the language that God uses in the Psalms and in the book of Romans to describe what humans who live in rebellion to God have become BECAUSE you were created with a purpose like the cup. What happens if the cup REFUSES to hold water and fulfill its purpose?

We have a joke in my house. My wife and kids laugh at me, but I do it to teach a lesson. A pen has one purpose; it was created for one and only reason, to write. So when I pick up a pen and it will not write, after giving it a fair chance, I dramatically look at that pen, and I speak out loud to it (this is where my family laughs), and I say to the pen, "Pen, you have one purpose. That's it. If you do not fulfill your purpose I have no use for you, into destruction you go." And I throw it in the trash because a pen that will not write is worthless. I get it when a pen runs out of ink; that doesn't aggravate me. The pen has fulfilled its purpose; it used its LIFE, but what drives me crazy is when a pen still has ink; it still has LIFE, but it is just being ornery. A sinner who is separated from Jesus Christ because he or she REFUSES to repent and bow to the rule of King Jesus, Lord of heaven and earth, is being stubborn, is being ornery. It's being like the pen that has life in it, but saying, "I refuse! I will NOT serve you! I'm my own pen, it's my life, it's my body."

But the follower of Christ is the person who has turned to God and said, “You made me, You own me, I bow. Jesus is Your Son? Then I bow to Him. He’s the Savior? Then I believe in Him. I want to come back and be Yours.” We belong to God; He owns us; He has the right over us just like a farmer owns an ox and has the right over the ox. He has the right to put us to work, but He has filled our life with blessing and gifts for enjoyment and goodness, so don’t get the wrong idea. But He has given us a purpose. He created us in His image, then spoke words of blessing and commissioning over us.

He gave us the task of bringing all things into harmony with the will of God. So that means, you; you are to bring yourself into harmony with the will of God. That means obedience. But it also means we are His agents of change in this world. For instance a child starving is NOT the will of God. So bring all things into harmony with the will of God. Feed that child. Disease running rampant, that’s not in harmony with God’s will, so heal the sick. People living without shelter, that’s not in harmony with God’s will, so house them. And then the biggest problem, this world is filled with people who are in rebellion to God. That’s the place of refusing to turn to Jesus Christ to be saved. God tells us that we have all sinned. If sin is not a big deal, then this is not a problem. But the Bible tells us that sin is a big deal to God. As big of a deal as if someone murdered your family, you don’t shrug your shoulders and say, “Just a mistake, no biggie.”

Sin is spitting in the face of a holy God. God is pure and clean and beautiful. His heaven is pure and clean and beautiful. Sin is maggot-crawling trash left out in the sun for a week in the summer. Sin is rancid to God. God will not allow any rancid thing into His kingdom of heaven or His presence. That's bad news because the Bible tells us that sin has made our hearts like the rancid maggot-filled trash. God tells us that our crimes deserve His punishment. Eternal, never-ending punishment in fact. God doesn't lie, and God doesn't exaggerate. If we stay separated from Him, we will suffer … only what we deserve, but what we deserve is hell.

But be so very grateful, your God is full of pity. He is full of compassion and mercy. And out of that pity and mercy, God sent His Son. Jesus lived a perfect life, keeping the law that we could not, being righteous. Then voluntarily gave Himself up to be delivered into the hands of wicked men who did their worst to Him. And in those moments of darkness on the cross, Jesus took my rancidness onto Himself and suffered for it. He died for my disgusting sins. He took the sins of God's people onto Himself and into the grave, then He burst through the doors of the tomb three days later showing His victory over sin, death, hell, Satan, and every effect of evil. He's beaten it!

And now He is declaring that all men everywhere should repent and be saved. This is also incredibly good news. To be delivered from the rebellion that you've made against God and freed from the punishment and given eternal life ("saved" is the word the Bible uses to describe all of that), you do not have to pay some amount of money or do enough good works to tip some imaginary scales. You turn to Jesus in faith and repentance. Faith being, to believe the facts, but not just that, to trust in Jesus. It is to believe the facts of Jesus' miraculous birth, believe that He died for sins and rose from the dead, but it is also to believe that He is Lord of heaven and earth.

If you believe He is Lord of heaven and earth, it is impossible for that not to change your life. If you believe He is Lord of heaven and earth, you will bow to Him. That's where repentance comes in. To repent is to turn. To decide to not follow your sin any longer, no longer just give in to it, you will not become perfect in a moment, that's later, but you decide you will not just give in to it, and you turn to Jesus with a resolve in your heart to obey Him. So it is the heart bowing to the authority of King Jesus. The Bible says, *"Whoever will call on the name of the Lord will be saved"* (Romans 10:13). Believe, repent, and God wants you to go to Him in prayer and call out to Him, tell Him you trust in Him and want to be saved.

This is what God wants of you, and yes, demands of you above all. That you turn to Jesus to be saved. Leave your rebellion and become a follower. God wants your worship. And this is the greatest crime that humanity has committed—leaving God.

So back to our flow of thought. Bring all things into harmony with the will of God. People are lost; people are separated from God; people are spiritually dead and on their way to destruction. No one is born a Christian; it has to be faith that you personally express in Him. It's not God's will that these remain in rebellion. So how do you be God's agent of change for this? Jesus' command to His people in what we call the Great Commission is: "Make disciples of all the nations." Tell people the message that we just looked at, the Bible calls that the "gospel" or the good news. When people hear the message of Christ, God makes that message supernaturally powerful. So God wants you to be a man who has conversations at work, conversations with friends, conversations with strangers at the grocery store, pointing people to Christ.

Bring all things into harmony with the will of God. When you have a wife, God wants you to lead her to walk with Him. If God gives you children, He wants you to gently guide them to Him, so that they are not rebels to God but see Him as amazing, as the God who is the source of all joy. When they want to follow Christ, then you've brought them into harmony with the will of God. This is your purpose. All things exist for the glory of God.

## 10) Real Men Imitate the Manliest Man

Why do we like the Rocky movies? Why does it make our hearts soar and dust get in our eyes when he goes the distance? Because there's something valiant about toughness, about endurance, about courage. What would you think of a man who set his face like flint to a cause that was noble, that saved lives, and along the way he got kicked in the teeth and knocked down, but he spit out the blood and stood back up? That's tough, that appeals to us.

I know that we are so used to the stories of the Bible that they all appear as coloring pages to us, but think about the reality of them. Jesus was thrown in the middle of a band of Roman soldiers who kicked the tar out of Him, but He stood up for more. In fact, before the crucifixion and even while it was happening, the Bible tells us that Jesus could have ended it all in a moment. He's God, just call down angels to destroy the soldiers and be done. But Jesus set His face like flint to go to the cross. The apostles even tried to talk Him out of it, but He wanted it. When He was being beaten and that cat-of-nine-tails was whipped across His back, lacerating the skin and exposing the ribs and the spine, Jesus never quit. He was offered wine on the cross to dull the pain; when He tasted what it was, He spit it back out because it was the Father's will for Him to feel every drop of the agony.

You want a picture of toughness and courage? There He is on the cross. Dying in my place, being a protector, being the Shepherd, who, in His death knocks the teeth out of the lion and the wolf. You want to see manliness? It has never been on display in more glory than Christ on the cross. And then three days later, kicking the teeth out of the final enemy—death itself. You want to be a man? Imitate Jesus, the God-man.

# 3

# Lust, and the Battle for Joy

1 Peter 2:11 says, *"Beloved, I urge you as aliens and strangers to abstain from fleshly lusts which wage war against the soul."* The Holy Spirit through Peter gives us the command to abstain from, notice it carefully, from lust, and then he tells us something about lust in our heart. It's important to notice that God doesn't just command us not to engage in actions. He tells us to fight the lust. Lust is the craving for indulgence, not the indulgence itself. We normally use the word "lust" only to talk about sexual lust, but in the Bible it refers to any craving that is ungodly.

God gives us certain desires that are to be controlled, but desires are not evil. The desire for food is not evil. When food is eaten with CONTENTMENT and GRATITUDE it's not evil. 1 Timothy 4:4, *"For everything created by God is good and nothing is to be rejected if it is received with gratitude."* In fact, we can worship God in that act. Having a heart filled with thanksgiving and basking in God's goodness while you enjoy that gift from God, that's giving Him glory.

And it also gives joy. Hear the word "joy" in the word "enJOY." Good desire, good gift, good enjoyment, God is glorified. But lust is different from that. Lust is wanting pleasure to a degree or in a way that is not honoring to God. We desire food, but even if we have to go without it, God calls us to be content. Because our joy isn't dependant on things; our joy is in God. He is the ultimate treasure. If we lived in a box and ate grass and bugs, so long as we had Christ, we're called to be content, and you really can be content and have joy. Paul wrote his letter to the Philippians from a prison cell, and the primary message of that book is to "Rejoice! What you have in Christ is so good, no matter what happens, no matter how much you suffer; if a persecutor is cutting off your fingers one by one while you watch, he can't do anything to your soul! It's secure in Christ!" Faith in those promises of God lets you have joy even when things in life aren't pleasant. Thus, be content.

But lust isn't content. Lust feels that I need this pleasure. It wants it in degrees, ways, or manners that God has not designed. God gave sex as a gift to be enjoyed within marriage. The desire is good; the gift is good; when it is enjoyed with contentment and gratitude, God is glorified. It's pure. But when a man lusts, his treasure is not in God, but in the pleasure itself. And lust creates a burning for that pleasure. And that lust is evil. It's not merely the actions that come from that lust, the lust itself is wicked in the heart.

## Lust Steals Joy

The point that Peter makes is that lust wages war against the soul. Lust does things to the soul that are destructive. Think about a 17-year-old boy. That 17-year-old boy is walking down the street and he sees a beautiful young girl. It is not evil to notice that she is beautiful, and I want to be careful here; don't use this as an excuse to lust with the eyes and call it good, but there is even a way to appreciate beauty as from God. The same way that we see the beauty of a sunset and admire God. But his reaction isn't that. He sees this young girl and lusts. What that lust is, is a dissatisfied craving. Dissatisfied. In other words, unfulfilled, non-glad craving. And the young man thinks to himself, "I wish I could see more of her." And the thought that is rooted down deep in the heart is, "If I could just see a little bit more, I would satisfied." So that young man walks to the beach. And there on the beach, he sees the same beautiful girl. And this time, she is wearing beach attire, and he sees a whole lot more of her.

Here's the question I have for you. In that moment, he is seeing what he wanted to see. Does his soul say, "Yes, now I'm content. I'm happy. That's all I wanted; I'll go home now"? No. Even more so, now that he has seen more of her, he is even more unsatisfied, and in his heart he wishes, "I want to see more of her." And the thought is down deep, "Then I would be happy."

So the young man leaves and goes to an establishment which has strippers. And he sees a beautiful woman wearing nothing. She's completely naked. Earlier he said, "I just want to see more, then I'd be happy." Well now he's seeing all of it. Does his soul say, "Yes, now I'm satisfied, that's all I wanted, now I'm happy"? No. Even more so, his body is now raging at this point. It is like a FIRE of unsatisfied desire burning inside of him. His heart, his mind, and his body are even *more unhappy* than when he began. He wants more so badly he can hardly contain himself. So let's say then that he visits a prostitute. And everything that he said that he wanted, is done. He has gratified his lust.

The question I have for you now is, does his soul have joy? Does his soul have rest; down in the depths of his spirit, is he satisfied? No. He doesn't have joy. Depending on the condition of his conscience, he might have extreme guilt. But even if his conscience has been seared and he doesn't have that guilt, that gratification has not left him with joy. And later, when the effects of this gratification are over, he will rage and burn even hotter at the temptation. He will be even more unsatisfied because he has fed his appetite. And feeding the appetites of the flesh make them burn even stronger. Here is the point. Sin and lust wage war against your joy. It promises satisfaction, and fulfillment and that "IT" that we all want, but it never, not once in all of history, has it ever given what it promises. In fact, it takes you farther away from it.

## Lust is Addictive

Every time lust is allowed to inhabit the heart, it digs its roots down deeper. Each time it gets harder and harder to fight, and easier and easier to give in to it. Indulging desires only intensifies its hold in a person's life. You do not have to have an addiction to a substance to know what addiction is. Like we said with the young man in the illustration, the next time he lusts, that lust is going to be even stronger. That's the way it works. Earlier we talked about actions, habits, and character in a good way, but it works the other way as well. The more wicked actions you engage in, the more it becomes habit. And the totality of your habits is your character; it's who you are; it becomes ingrained into your life. You look at porn over and over; eventually that becomes a part of your character. And all of that sin robs your joy. If you hate someone, the next time you're going to hate even harder. If you gratify your coveting by buying whatever you want, each time you do that, the impulse gets stronger. You don't satisfy the cravings by feeding it! Feeding lusts only make them stronger! Saying yes to sin is dangerous!

## Sin and Lust Take You Further Than You Ever Intended

Sin and lust always take you further than you intended to go. That illustration with the young man spells it out. Lust of the eyes is never content to stay—lust of the eyes. Jesus said in Matthew 5 that looking on a woman with lust for her is adultery in the heart. Have you ever thought about why? Let me ask you, is lust of the eyes ever content to just do that? No. It's not gratified until it acts on it. It's not gratified until it takes her and lays with her. The same with hatred. Is hatred ever content? No. Hatred is a lusting for violence. It's not satisfied until it murders. That's what it wants. Lust wants adultery, and hatred wants murder. Hatred is just murder in its seed form.

Lust is always pushing you to go further than you want to go. We get into a sin and think in the heart, "I'll only go this far, and then I'm going to stop." But every time, without fail, it pushes you further than you ever thought you would go. Rapist after rapist would tell you from their prison cell, they never intended to be a rapist, it began with pornography. The slow progression is unnoticeable unless you're looking for it.

## Sin Inhibits Your Capacity for Joy

Sin robs your soul of its ability to feel pleasure. It only feels fixes and temporary satisfactions. Enjoying a good pleasure gives clean enjoyment, but what happens in fleshly pleasure? What happens with too much food? It becomes dull. If you want an experiment, do this, go eat a gallon of ice cream. If a little bit is good, a whole lot is great, right? Go eat a gallon of ice cream. The first five minutes is going to be enjoyable. But by the time you've put down half that gallon, the taste has gone dull, the pleasure diminishes, and eventually turns into misery.

What about sleep? Same thing. The good gift gives enjoyment, overdo it, and the pleasure leaves, and eventually becomes horrible. It's the law of diminishing returns. When lust is raging unchecked in your body, you lose the ability to enjoy, because it's never enough! You have to keep going further.

But now do this experiment. Fast for three days. At the end of those three days take a bite of bread. What you will experience in that moment is amazing! That bread will be the sweetest thing you have ever put in your mouth. What's the principle? For enjoyment to be good, it has to be managed. Self-control is necessary for joy.

If you abuse pleasure you can come to a place where you no longer enjoy. You can come to a place where food is no longer enjoyable. It's all dull. You can come to a place where sex is no longer enjoyable. It is a known issue in the counseling circles, that some men who get engrossed in pornography cannot even make love to their wives anymore. They have to open a dirty magazine to get aroused, and keep it open and look at it during sex. Boy, I bet that wife feels beautiful, but what a horrifying thought! Where simple pleasures like music, and breezes, and sunsets don't matter to you because your soul gets calloused. The capacity for joy has been diminished.

## Self Control

You need to discipline your body, your mind, your eyes, and your heart. Your body lusts and craves for things that are not right until you're married. Do not allow yourself to give in to them. If you have a girlfriend, your body feels the desire to have sex with her. You be a man of discipline, and you keep your desires in check. The day will come when those desires will find their fulfillment, but it is not now. This is a matter of joy and misery, and it can even be a matter of life and death, and much more importantly—a matter of eternity.

You make the commitment, the vow to God, that you will not have sex with a woman until you have taken her to be your wife. And even if you decide that you will not have sex before you are married, you may be tempted to engage in some touching and "fooling around," but do not do it. You discipline yourself to be a man of integrity and honor. Somewhere out there is your future wife, do you want some random guy touching her in places that are supposed to be reserved for you and you alone? Of course not. If you haven't married her then her body isn't yours, so hands off.

Make a commitment not to put yourself in a position of temptation. Don't go park and then crawl into the backseat as if you don't know what's going to happen. Keep your relationship pure. Talk about it with your girlfriend. If she's not on the same page with you on this issue, she is not the girl for you, so move on. Discipline your body.

But Jesus even goes further in this area. Jesus tells us in the Sermon on the Mount, *"You have heard that it was said, "You shall not commit adultery"; but I say to you that everyone who looks at a woman with lust for her has already committed adultery with her in his heart."* Christ is telling you that you need to discipline your eyes. All sin can be divided into three categories—the lust of the flesh, the lust of the eyes, and the boastful pride of life.

What's hard for us to grasp is that one whole category of sin is lust of the eyes. Our culture hasn't really seen anything wrong with lusting with the eyes. In fact that's the primary thing that advertising depends on. But remember the 10th commandment—*You shall not covet.* God commands us not to look on ANY object and crave it. It's not wicked to recognize beauty, but it is wrong to covet it, to yearn for it, whether it's a Corvette or a woman. So as men of integrity Christ calls us to discipline our eyes. In the book of Job he tells us that he made a covenant with his eyes not to look on a woman with lust.

What is even more astounding is that Jesus told us that command about not looking on a woman with lust in a day when women wore full length robes! Today, you go to your local mall and you will see girls with shorts so short their cheeks are hanging out, low-riding to reveal their whale-tail, v-neck tops going so low you see all but the nipple. Yeah, it's harder to keep pure eyes in this culture. But God put you here and God doesn't put you in situations that are hopeless. You can do it. He promises to give you grace. What you've got to learn to do is discipline those eyes. Here's how you start; make the commitment to look a woman only in the eyes. When an attractive woman walks past you, intentionally look the opposite direction. If she walks to the left of you, turn your head to the right. As a Christian, other people are going to look to see what your eyes do. Make it obvious.

Somewhere out there is the woman you're going to marry. Do you like the idea of dirty old men looking her up and down, undressing her with their eyes? No, that's disgusting. Right now she belongs to her father; she is still under his protection, and one day she will be yours. All yours and you don't have to share. Her body, every beautiful curve will be yours. Just the same as your body will belong to her (1 Cor 7:4). Here's the point, if you look at another woman with lustful eyes, you're looking at another man's wife. You're taking something that you don't have the right to take.

On this same note, absolutely do not allow your eyes to look on pornography in any form. Guys, I cannot stress this enough; every image you look on is going to rape your mind. I have known friends, and I have known pastors absolutely get addicted to pornography. It has the power to grab hold of your heart. I have known men who couldn't think of anything else, it is so powerful it can take over your life.

Many scientific studies have been done in this area, but they all essentially say what Scripture teaches. The effect of pornography is nothing short of catastrophic. One particular study is disturbing. At the beginning of the study men were exposed to a pornographic movie that depicted women being brutally raped and beaten. They measured the men's heart rates in response to this repulsive image. The first time they saw this, their heart rates jumped as a natural response of disgust. But then the men were subjected to six weeks of daily pornographic material, not violent, just regular pornography. They brought the men in after the six weeks and exposed them to another movie clip of a woman being brutally raped and beaten. What they found was absolutely shocking, though not surprising. The men's heart rates were significantly lower than the first time they were exposed. Meaning, what ought to have shocked them to disgust, just wasn't that disgusting to them anymore.

Young men, hear the call here. Pornography is not harmless! It is dangerous. It will affect your heart and your mind for the rest of your life. You have access to it right at your fingertips, but you have got to resist. If you already find yourself immersed in this and you don't think you can quit, go talk to your pastor. I know that sounds frightening, but a good pastor is going to show you grace and help you thru this. But even if it is embarrassing, this is about your life. Repent and leave it.

Next, you need to discipline your mind, your thoughts. You are going to be tempted to carry on fantasies, but this you must also resist. In 2 Corinthians 10:4, Paul says that thru his work of the gospel he is laboring to take *every thought captive to the obedience of Christ.* It's not stated as a command, but see the obvious command inherit in that verse. Take every thought captive to obedience to Christ. Do not allow even a thought of sin to linger in your mind. Get it out of your mind as quickly as possible. The longer it stays the more power it will have over you.

Here's what Jesus has to say right after he calls us not to look with lust. *"If your right eye makes you stumble, tear it out and throw it from you; for it is better for you to lose one of the parts of your body, than for your whole body to be thrown into hell. If your right hand makes you stumble, cut it off and throw it from you; for it is better for you to lose one of the parts of your body, than for your whole body to go into hell.* Jesus says to remove from your life anything that causes you to sin. It is a matter of eternity—heaven and hell. He is not saying that you get to heaven by being good enough, avoiding enough sin, or doing enough good works. But He does teach us this, to be saved you must believe and repent.

Repentance means turning your back on sin. It means to leave it. Not become perfect, but leave it. It is possible to love a sin so much you refuse to leave it. It is possible to be so attached that it keeps you from truly turning to God in your heart. Just ask the rich young ruler. He loved his money so much, he couldn't leave it. If you have to break up with your girlfriend or throw away your TV, you do it. Better to have eternal life. Of course, if you'll discipline your life before it gets to this point, you won't have to worry about those drastic measures.

# 4

# Dating and How to Treat a Lady

Knowing what we've learned so far, how should a young man treat a young lady? First of all God commands men to treat ALL women with purity. You are to regard every believing woman as a sister in Christ and interact with her in purity and a sense of protection because she is part of the family of God. Unbelieving women are to be treated with grace and with a desire to see them repent and turn to Christ. All are to be regarded with purity; with your eyes, your heart, and your body. But the point of this chapter is in regard to a young man captivated with a girl romantically.

So how should a young man regard her and treat her? What you are aiming for is an attitude, not merely actions, but the heart. You give a woman flowers and say, "Here, it's Valentine's Day; it's my duty; it's what I'm supposed to do," with a mechanical tone in your voice, and you are going to communicate, "I don't really care for you; I'm just trying to get by with what I *have* to do." That does not communicate affection. Affection delights to bless her. Love rejoices in the beloved. So what you want to communicate with your body language, the look in your eyes, the tone in your voice, and the actions you perform to serve her, is that you want to bless her. But here are some of the "rules" to keep in mind for how you ought to treat this girl you are romancing. When you do these with a right heart, with affection in your soul, these things will communicate care for her. It would be easy to just fly through this section just to get it read, but slow down and pay attention to each point. "Little things" often mean the greatest difference for a girl.

Open doors for her. Remember the call to sacrificially serve? This comes in to play. It is not a woman's job to open doors for you; you take the initiative and treat her like she is special to you.

If you are sitting when she approaches, stand to show her honor. Remember 1 Peter 3:7, a husband is to show his wife honor as a fellow heir of the grace of life. Also, stand when she is leaving. In fact, this is a good rule of thumb for anyone who approaches—if in doubt, just stand. It communicates humble respect.

When she is speaking, look her in the eyes. Not only will this be meaningful to her and help stir affection in her for you, but remember the previous instruction. Do not be looking at her body or let your eyes drift to her chest. Give her your full attention. Stop whatever else is going on. If you're watching TV, turn away from it, and give her your complete concentration. The only exception is when you're driving, you are allowed to look at the road.

If there is a situation where there are not enough seats, be sure to give up your seat to her. And even beyond just the woman you are seeking to woo, this is a principle for all ladies present in a room. When you're in a restaurant waiting to be seated, and there are only so many chairs, don't you dare sit down while a woman has to stand, even if it's not your woman. Have a sense of nobility. Stand up, walk over to the woman, and say "Ma'am, there's a seat for you right over there." Do that one time and watch what happens. First, you might feel a little uneasy about it, but you'll notice after that, oftentimes it causes other men to do the same. The bums will keep sitting, but other men to whom nobility matters will follow suit. Have a sense of honor in these things; it's about godly masculinity.

Help her into her seat. Pull her chair out for her (No, not out from under her, but out for her).

When you're walking, don't rush ahead of her and leave her behind. Walk at a pace that will accommodate her speed. Also, a throwback from the days of horse and carriage, a man should walk on the side between her and the road. What this did in times past was protect the woman from mud splashing up or even a horse that veered off course. It's still a practice that demonstrates protection to a woman. No, you're probably not going to stop an oncoming car with your brute strength, but there's an attitude of protection present.

When you speak to her, don't speak to her like she's just one of the guys. Speak to her with gentleness. Save brashness for the guys, address her like a lady.

When you are standing in a group, be sure not to crowd her out behind you. Step back so she can be included in the circle.

When it's raining, find an umbrella for her. If you are arriving at a destination in the rain, pull up to the front, politely ask her to stay put, jump out and open the door for her, and hold the umbrella over her body.

Help her take her coat off when appropriate. Help her put it on when it is time to leave. She will notice this act of gentlemanliness.

Never let her, or any woman in your group for that matter, carry items when your arms are empty. When it's possible, you be the pack-mule. And if the both of you are carrying items, you choose the heavier ones.

If you are standing in line, let her go ahead of you.

When you speak to her parents, do so with a polite attitude of submissive confidence. Shake her father's hand and look him in the eyes. Assure him with your demeanor that you are an honorable man and that your intentions are pure. Avoiding eye contact is going to leave him wondering if you are hiding something. And remember the part about being submissive. Before you marry this girl, she belongs to her father, she's not yours. You may only see her by his permission. Don't get aggressive with him and try to dominate conversations or act bigger than what you are. Lower yourself beneath his authority and let that be known by your body language.

When you're out together and you see someone you know, introduce her to them. It's considered rude to talk to someone and not tell them who she is to you. It will make her feel like she's not important to you. Introducing her will make her feel special.

When you're together, sit tall with good posture. I know this sounds picky, and I know slouching is common, but it presents an attitude of disrespect. It gives the impression that you don't care what she has to say. So many ways we communicate are nonverbal. Subconsciously we read someone's body language and come to conclusions. Make sure that your body language, your facial expressions, your eye contact, and even the tone of your voice communicate that you are excited to be with her, that you count this a privilege, and that you are interested in what she has to say.

When you ask her on a date, ask her confidently and politely. There are right ways and wrong ways to ask a girl out. "So dude, I'm going to McDonald's tomorrow; you should come along," doesn't exactly depict the fairy-tale princess fantasies she's entertained in her mind. Asking a girl out via text message is cowardly. I advise girls to respond to those texts in this way. "When you are man enough to ask me to my face, I will consider it." Look at her with *confidence* and tell her you would like to take her out and spend some time with her. But give her the opportunity to say "no." Many young men are eager to press and guilt a girl into saying "yes." But if she does not want to go with you; she's not right for you, and all that leads to are broken hearts and even miserable marriages.

If she says "no," respect her wishes. I'm not saying don't be persistent (my wife turned me down several times over the course of two years). If she's showing signs she's interested in you and you have a friendship, then by all means, continue to be friends and see if it progresses. But you've got to know when to back off. Having four younger sisters I saw my fair share of young men who couldn't take a hint. My sisters were not interested in a particular man, nor would they ever be, but the young man just wouldn't drop it. At that point you become the creepy stalker guy; don't be the creepy stalker guy.

At the end of all that, hear this. These are all examples of situations, but really you're going to express affection to her in just the normal stuff of life. The tone of your voice when you ask her for a pen reveals the way you regard her in your heart. Let kindness, grace, and affection rule the way you speak to her, treat her, and act towards her.

Most likely the time will come when you realize you need to break up with a girl. When this is being done remember this; a girl typically invests much more of her heart into a relationship than a young man does. If you've been dating, she's most likely already dreamed about your wedding. What that means is, this is going to hurt her. Resist the temptation to take the coward's way out. No text break-ups! It really needs to be done to her face. Man up, and gently tell her that you do not think you two are good together. Don't lie to her and give her false hope; don't make up any ridiculous excuses; tell her the truth, but be gentle.

## Wooing Her

Now that you know how to properly treat a girl, what about dating or courtship? Call it what you want, but for a godly young man here's the intention. God has wired you and her up so that when you spend good time together your affections will increase; your exhilaration over one another will grow, and it will brew into a desire to be together. Which is great if this is the girl you want to be with, but if you're dating just to be dating, you're going to have affections stirred for someone who's not right for you. Which is why you've got to be careful about who you date and how much time you spend together. But assuming you have a godly, pure girl who is a delight to you, here's what you're trying to do in dating. You are seeking to woo her.

Wooing her is when you melt her heart; it's when you help stir the affections in her heart for yourself. You are seeking to romance her. Now let me be clear. Only do these things if you intend to do it for life. If you pretend to be a gentleman to capture her heart only so you can score, that is repulsive and manipulative. That's not honorable, it's disgusting. And you're also not trying to woo her only to marry her and then treat her like dirt. If you do that—you are lying. Learn how to woo this woman so you can keep wooing her for the rest of your life. This is not how to fool a lady, it's how to treat a lady for life. I'm not trying to help you score, I'm trying to help you be a blessing to the woman you will keep loving till the end. The goal is not to manipulate her, but to serve her. You will manipulate her if you only woo her to try to get something. But if out of love you want to bring gladness to her, that's just blessing her. You may not like Italian restaurants, but if she digs them, then you're blessing her to take her there. That's honorable, but manipulating her, playing her, or using her is not; it's just shameful.

The fact is you can manipulate many girls. If you pretend well enough and play the game, you can manipulate girls into feeling affection for you to the point where they give their bodies to you. But it is disgusting, and there's nothing honorable about that. You want to woo a girl for the intention of moving towards marriage. If you can't see yourself marrying this girl then why in the world are you dating her?! Dating is not for entertainment. This is too big of a deal to waste time with someone who is not right for you, and it is too big of a deal to play around with.

When you find that girl and you want to woo—study her; think about her (in the right way). Go slow on this one.

After one or two dates it's probably not the time to serenade her outside her window, but after six months, maybe. So slowly study her. Study her face. When you give her a gift, what happens with her eyes? Do they light up? What about when you sing to her? Does her heart melt? Find out the things that woo her. To do that you've got to try a lot of stuff. Some ideas are going to bomb; others are going to move her.

When you're planning time to spend together, get creative. Go for a hike; take her fishing; go for a boat ride while you paddle; picnic by the lake; grill out together; go to a football game; work out together. If you're not outdoorsy and active then you're on your own, but you get the point. Find out her favorite activities and plan a Saturday afternoon to do them with her. Yeah, you ought to do the dinner and a movie thing, but also be spontaneous as well.

There's nothing that says you have to plan everything, but there's a leadership principle at play here. Simply picking her up and saying, "What do you want to do?" is fine once in a while, but you'll show love and leadership if you try to plan things that will be fun for her.

## What About Physical Contact?

You've seen from Scripture that it is wickedness before God to engage in sexual union before you're married, but what about other physical contact? What's appropriate, what's not? Here's what you need to do. You need to decide what you believe is honorable. If Jesus was this girl's Father, and you were engaged to be married, and you asked Him, "How much may I touch Your daughter, how far am I allowed to go?" What do you think He would answer? Whatever that answer is, that's what will honor God.

I'm a father, so let me be honest. I believe that you may hold her hand, and if it gets serious, you may kiss her. Not lying down kissing in the back of a car, but kiss. The hands need to stay where they will not be tempted to touch anything you don't have the right to until she's your wife. Again, this is a matter of honor. Do what's right. When you're married, she's yours, but until then there are boundaries. Set those boundaries and absolutely do not cross them. That means you need to make resolves about what you will and will not do on dates. Don't go park your car in the middle of the boondocks "just to talk." You know what you're going to be tempted to do when that happens. Make plans ahead of time while you're thinking clearly because in the moment, when you're with her and your affections are stirred and the flesh is raging, you don't make wise decisions. Plan to obey God, then control yourself to follow through. Conduct yourself honorably; treat her like a lady; woo her heart.

As things continue to morally spiral downwardly in our culture, it is absolutely disgusting how girls are being treated. Now granted, they're bringing a lot of it on themselves. A girl who dresses like a prostitute is going to be treated like one. When she dresses like her body is for sale, she shouldn't be surprised when men only want her body and care nothing about her heart.

But why is she acting that way? Very often it is because she has a father who is not guarding her, not giving her attention that she needs. So she may wreck her life sleeping with man after man, finally having kids, where they will be raised to see life the same way. Do you see how this will be an endless cycle of misery? The only way to stop it is to change the course. You, as a young man pursuing honor, you've got to be about something different. Decide that you're not going to be a part of that cycle. Commit to yourself that you're going to treat women in a way that honors Christ. Keep yourself pure; keep your intentions pure; and keep your relationships pure. Have a sense of honor in these things.

I can guarantee, if you go to a public school and you conduct yourself like this, you are going to get made fun of in the locker room. The guys are going to think you are a wuss. And it won't just be light-hearted fun, in a mean-spirited way they are going to deride you. Go ahead and plan on it happening. And go ahead and decide that their approval isn't worth dishonoring God. Better to be mocked, better to get beat up, better to die than to disobey the Lord. You stay honorable, and your reward will be waiting. Some of it now, but definitely in the kingdom to come.

# 5

# Choosing a Wife

Here are the facts. That girl who wears the jeans so low you can see the whale-tail, the v-neck cut so deep you can see her belly-button ring, that girl that stirs those feelings in you that makes you want to be with her, yeah—those feelings, that's the flesh. That's the lust of the eyes and the lust of the flesh taking over. That girl, that's the girl who will be married three times by the age of 40 and each marriage ended with adultery. You be with her, and you'll be one of the men in her path of destruction. Used and left behind. That girl who lives fast and smokes and drinks, there's an ugly future awaiting her. Literally.

I'm telling you right now, next time you get a chance, take a stroll through a local bar. (I know, you may not be 21, and even when you are 21, a bar is really not a place where much of any good is going to happen. But maybe on your way to the family area, stroll close to that door and look in there). Here's what you'll see. Oh you'll see some twenty-year-old women seducing men and looking nice. But take a look at the 40-year-old women in that bar. What do you see? You will see some of the grisliest, foul-mouthed females on the planet. That smoke has taken that soprano voice and made it croak like a frog; that drinking has put some serious sagging in her face, and the hard living has taken some years off her life already. (Not to mention what manner of venereal diseases she may be harboring).

Now, visit a good church (emphasis on "good") in your area that preaches the gospel and faithfully teaches even the hard parts of God's Word, and take a look at some of the good healthy marriages there, the ones who have been walking with the Lord for years. What do those 30- and 40-year-old women look like? Most of the time it's not the riveting beauty of a 20 year old, but you will see a light in her eyes. You will see a woman who will still be a joy to look on at that age.

Here's my point. That rough sinful living often times has a way of showing its effects. Are looks everything? Absolutely not. But come on. The outer beauty of a woman is not everything, but see the obvious point here. You've got a choice. That smoking, drinking, sleeping-around, hard-living woman is going to age quickly and bring misery to every man she destroys. Yeah it's different in Hollywood, I know, but they pay tens of thousands of dollars on plastic surgery to get that ugliness erased away. And yeah, we're all going to get old and wrinkly, no matter who you marry, but I would much rather my 40-year-old wife look like she's 40, instead of 70. You keep a woman joyful, fulfilled, feeling beautiful, enriched, and walking with the Lord, and you've got a recipe for many more years of beauty.

Thus—be wise in who you allow yourself to be attracted to. Be wise in who you go out with, and be wise in the kind of girl you pursue.

Listen again to 1 Peter 3:1-6 as God calls women to holiness. *"In the same way, you wives, be submissive to your own husbands so that even if any of them are disobe-*

*dient to the word, they may be won without a word by the behavior of their wives, as they observe your chaste and respectful behavior. Your adornment must not be merely external—braiding the hair, and wearing gold jewelry, or putting on dresses; but let it be the hidden person of the heart, with the imperishable quality of a gentle and quiet spirit, which is precious in the sight of God. For in this way in former times the holy women also, who hoped in God used to adorn themselves, being submissive to their own husbands; just as Sarah obeyed Abraham, calling him lord, and you have become her children if you do what is right without being frightened by any fear."*

Notice some of the qualities to look for in a godly wife. # 1 at the top of the list—choose a believer. 2 Corinthians 6:14 says, *"Do not be bound together with unbelievers; for what partnership have righteousness and lawlessness, or what fellowship has light with darkness."* Literally that phrase do not be bound together is—do not be unequally yoked. That's terminology from the Old Testament that the Holy Spirit applies to us in this New Covenant. An oxen and a donkey were not to be yoked together (that is, attached together) to plow a field. God gave that command, as with many other commands in the Law of Moses, specifically to teach a truth through an illustration, and it is no longer about oxen and donkeys but to teach a timeless principle.

And the principle that God makes clear in 2 Corinthians 6 is, a believer is not to be united together with an unbeliever. So if you are a Christian young man you are not to pursue a relationship with a young woman who is lost. And really, if your heart is right, you're not going to be interested in that unbeliever. That woman who has rejected Christ is an enemy of God! Now you might reason, "Well maybe she's just never heard the gospel." By all means, go share the gospel with her. If she repents, turns to Christ in faith, and then shows fruit, then proceed. But if not, you will regret being with her. And Never, Ever, under any circumstances—date a girl and tell yourself, "Well I'll lead her to Christ through our dating." Flirt to convert. Listen, God is gracious and every once in a while that works out, but all you have to do is speak to enough Christians and you will hear a sad story. They tried it, it did not work, and they fell in love, and now they are in a miserable marriage to an unbeliever who treats him or her horribly, but they are stuck. They wish they had never gone down that road. This is too big of a deal to take gambles like that. Speak to yourself the rule, only pursue a follower of Christ.

Also from the 1 Peter 3 passage, notice the discussion of beauty. Our culture is very confused on this subject. God created beauty. Beauty in this world is something that displays God's glory, and He enjoys it. In Song of Solomon we see that it is a good thing to delight in the beauty of your wife. But we also have to understand that outward beauty pales in comparison to the weight of importance of a woman's inner beauty. Vastly more important than her dress dimensions is the purity of her heart. I know this may sound a little "After-School-Special" to you but in all seriousness, this is about your joy. You should be attracted to your wife, and really you won't be interested in a woman if you're not physically attracted to her, but you need to put a much greater weight on the kind of person she is. Many men go after a girl because she's hot, but then it turns out later that, she may be hot, but she's also repulsively cruel and a selfish hag who nags her husband relentlessly, and they end up being miserable. Don't get so wrapped up in looks that you don't evaluate her soul.

God calls a wife to be submissive to her husband; you've got to try to determine, this girl you're interested in, is she the kind of woman who would respect you? Or is she the kind of woman who would try to rule over you? Does she have a genuine love for Christ or does she just go through the motions of church? Genuine beauty is a purity in the soul. Look for a girl who serves others. Look for a girl who loves children. That girl who doesn't want to hold a baby and doesn't want to play with toddlers, that is a self-absorbed woman. That high-maintenance girl is going to be hard to live with. Look for a girl who's more concerned about her walk with God than her makeup.

Remember this, you only want to be in love with one woman in your life. You don't want to go through a series of relationships, "falling in love" with each one of them. Protect your affections. Don't let yourself fall crazy like Romeo. Romeo was a sissy, bawling and rolling around whining about loving a woman and then the next day falling for another girl. That's not nobility, that's not honor. Protect your heart and your love until you see this is going somewhere.

## Meant to be?

You have a choice in who you are going to be with, so choose wisely. A lot of times Christians really get confused on this whole issue. Christians will often say in regard to a certain relationship when someone questions it, "Well I think it's just meant to be." Which very well may be true, but you also need to understand that it *was meant to be* for Judas to betray Jesus. What he did was God's will, God's secret will, that is. That's the same kind of will in which Pharaoh did God's will, by having a hard heart and bringing catastrophe on himself, his family, and his nation. God has two wills. He has His revealed will and then His secret will. His revealed will is what He tells you to do. His secret will is what He brings about by His sovereign plan. It was God's secret will for Judas to betray Jesus, for Pharaoh to be arrogant, and for Kim Kardashian to marry Kris Humprey. But in none of those cases was it good for those involved. That's not the way God calls you to make decisions, to try to figure out His secrets. God calls you to use wisdom, discretion, insight, your brain. But so many times Christians just do whatever they want and claim, "Well it happened, so it must have been God's will." By that logic just go jump in front of a bus, But you know better than that. That would be idiotic, use wisdom.

# 6

# Real Love

In 1 Corinthians 13:4-8, God gives us a definition of what real godly love is. Listen to how the Holy Spirit through the apostle Paul defines it. *"Love is patient, love is kind and is not jealous; love does not brag and is not arrogant, does not act unbecomingly; it does not seek its own, is not provoked, does not take into account a wrong suffered, does not rejoice in unrighteousness, but rejoices with the truth; bears all things, believes all things, hopes all things, endures all things. Love never fails."* You're probably familiar with this passage, but here's one of the points that's interesting about it—God is not talking about romantic love here. It applies to romantic love as well, but this is even how you are to love the people in your church. The kind of love that is described in this passage is *agape* love. See, our English word "love" is used to refer to a lot of different things; whereas, in Greek (the original language the New Testament was written in) they used a different word for different kinds of love and affection. So for instance, the love that a brother has for a sister, a familial love is the Greek word *phileo* (where we get our English word "Philadelphia," the city of brotherly love). A sexual kind of lust was known as *eros* (where we get our English word "erotic"). But this word *agape* was used of pure love, the kind of love that God shows towards His children. It's holy, it's good, it's pure, it's Christ-like. And it's also very different from the understanding of love from our culture.

We will often say something like, "I love ice cream." But think about that, what are we saying when we make that statement? We're saying, "I enjoy what ice cream does for me. It makes me happy. It indulges my desires." There's nothing about that kind of affection that is *agape*. Real love is 1 Corinthians 13. It's focusing your attention not on yourself, but on blessing this person who is the object of your love.

Maybe the most important phrase in the definition that 1 Corinthians 13 gives is in verse 5, *"It does not seek its own."* When a boy tells his girlfriend, "If you don't have sex with me I'm not going to love you," love is not even on the radar screen in his heart. Not real love, anyway. He doesn't have love for that girl; he has lust; dirty, unclean lust. Real unconditional love is just that, unconditional. It's not based on anything that is done for you; it's based on the fact that you have chosen to set your love on this person. When God sets His love on His children, He doesn't stop loving us if we don't give Him what He wants. Even when we're faithless, He continues to faithfully love us. Love is a devotion, a commitment to bless this person with our words, our actions, and yes, with our affections.

Love is not merely a feeling. Now understand this, there has to be feelings and emotions involved for it to be love. If you feel nothing, then it's not love. But those feelings are called "affections." So, often when chick-flicks talk about "falling in love" what they really mean is that affections are growing in their heart. Which is part of love, but it is not all of it. Real love commits to keep blessing her even when she's cruel to you. Real love remains devoted to her even if she is in an accident and loses the ability to meet any of your needs. And real love keeps rekindling those affections even after 50 years of marriage.

Here's what's even more enlightening about what real love is. God originally gave the commands for a husband to love his wife and for a wife to love and respect her husband at a time when arranged marriages were not uncommon! In the Old Testament we see several times when arranged marriages took place. Today we're shocked at that notion. "How could they know if they're compatible? What if they didn't love each other?" Those are all modern questions. What that proves is this, even if your parents chose a wife for you, and she was, well, not so hot and not so great, you're still commanded to love her! You are still commanded to feel affection for her. You are still commanded to delight yourself in her. That means, this whole obsession with finding "the one" and "being compatible" is just more modern nonsense.

Do I believe that God has one girl for you to marry? Yes. Do I believe you should find someone you're compatible with? Yes. But I also know that we mess things up a lot of times, and regardless of where you find yourself, you're called to love. If an arranged marriage can have joy, love, delight, romance, and passion as Isaac and Rebekah's did in Genesis, then it's still possible today. But it will only come when we GET OVER OURSELVES and focus all of our attention and affection on her. If it's selfish, then it isn't love.

All of that is so crucial to understanding what God has designed for marriage. A very common phrase that people give today for why they divorce is that they "fell out of love." One thing is for sure, they never understood what love is to begin. Love keeps pursuing, love never fails. It is easy when it is all new and fresh for love to be invigorating, to do what Proverbs 5 commands, to be drunk on each other's love. One can't help it when it's new. But after time it gets harder for things to be fresh, for the affections to soar like they once did so easily. But God has commanded husbands and wives to keep pursuing one another and to delight themselves in one another.

Love takes work! Just like joy takes work. It's easy to have joy when someone gives you a new car or you win a football game. But God commands you to have joy even when you are in a prison cell for preaching the gospel and your torturers are cutting off your fingers one by one while you watch. How do you have joy then? You fight for it. You have control over your heart; you have control over your emotions, and you have control over your affections.

A godly marriage is a marriage that keeps re-stirring the affections for one's beloved—keeps romancing, keeps pursuing one another, keeps dating, keeps wooing, and keeps refocusing affections. Very often what happens in the world is that a man and woman lust for each other with passion, get married, and when it's no longer easy, divorce. Then they both go on to do the same thing with other people. But a godly marriage puts in work, and as time passes their love doesn't diminish, it only grows in its depth.

Listen young men, it really does get better. That's not just poetic, it really does. But I can see as I look around at other marriages and observe my own, it ONLY gets better for the ones that do the work. The marriages that get lazy, while they may stay together, husband and wife just end up being roommates. No passion, no intimacy, little sex, and very little joy. But the marriages that work hard God's way, that read Song of Solomon often, and put into practice its principles, the sex only gets better, the love only gets deeper, the affection gets richer. I'm not going to lie, it is different than the honeymoon. The honeymoon stage is a special time that God gives as a gift, and it doesn't stay for life, but a new kind of depth grows. And it's good. Real good.

# 7

# Marriage and Sex

My wife and I began dating when we were 15. We had one break-up when we were 16, got back together after a couple months, and then I made her my wife when we were 21. We dated from age 15 to age 21, the peak of testosterone rage. But we waited to come together sexually until we were married. Full disclosure, we were not a model of purity. We went too far when it came to making out and all the touching that can come, but we were resolute to wait until we were married to have sex.

I had made a vow to God to remain a virgin until my wedding night. So for six years I dated this smoking-hot young woman who became a college athlete, and by the time our wedding night came, our bodies were burning for each other. And this is what I want to tell you young men. I'm more than ten years into my marriage right now, and that burning that we felt for one another that built up from waiting, it hasn't left. And it's good, I mean—Real Good.

But this is what I hear from almost every unbelieving man who shares details with me about their marriage, either privately or, you know how it is when a group of unbelieving men get together, they share it all. I continually hear these men talk about how their wives won't ever have sex with them. What so often happens is that a couple has sex before they are married, and by the time they're married, there's really nothing to look forward to. One couple boasted to a group of friends that on their wedding night they were just so tired from the day they just decided to go to sleep.

My wife and I looked at each other with a smirk. I can tell you right now, that wasn't what happened on my wedding night! All that time of loving each other and waiting, on our honeymoon, it was absolutely amazing. I'm not just talking about the physical, but the connection down deep to the soul. And on our honeymoon we told each other that we were so glad we waited. And ten years later, I'm still more thankful than I've ever been that we waited. After ten years we are still feeling the benefits of waiting. After a decade, the benefits of waiting are still resonating.

So the couples who went ahead and had sex, maybe in the backseat of a car, hiding from their parents, who stole away for twenty minutes and had to hurry up, they spoiled it. And now, sex has become boring to them. Kind of like how your grandma used to warn you about spoiling supper. When you get hungry, really hungry, and you don't want to wait you may grab a couple cookies. And you think to yourself, "This will just hold me over till supper." But after you eat the cookies, you sit, you wait, and when it's time to eat you find, you're not hungry anymore. The appetite is gone. You want to enjoy a big meal with all its deliciousness, but the cookies spoiled it. This is what happens when sex is engaged in before marriage. It spoils it. And especially for ladies, they sit down for the meal, but their appetite is gone.

That is always the way sin goes. Temptation builds in your flesh; you feel this heavy lusting and craving within you that wants immediate gratification. So you give in, only to then be very disappointed and left feeling guilty afterwards. And very often the sin eventually gets boring. It's called "the law of diminishing returns." You play Atari and everyone thinks it's awesome, but then Nintendo comes out and all of a sudden that Atari gets pretty boring, so you have to move on to something new.

This is what happens when men look at pornography. At first just a simple picture is exciting, but then after looking at those simple pictures for a while, it gets normal. So he goes to find racier pictures. And for a little while that's exciting. But then, even that gets boring. This continues on and on, the pictures have to be raunchier and cruder, until finally, pictures aren't enough. That's when you get Ted Bundy. But even when it doesn't progress that far (but there are prisons full of young men who never meant to go as far as the did), our culture has no shortage of men who have affairs because they've gotten bored with sex with their wife. And so for more pleasure, they throw away everything.

But that crazy train is the cycle of sin. The marriages who obey the Lord are the happiest on the planet. But it certainly doesn't happen automatically because you are a Christian. As a child of God you have access to more grace, more power from heaven, more help from God than anyone else. But not every Christian walks by the Spirit and receives those gifts that God offers. You have a part to play in it. And the part you play is effort and obedience and prayer, and if you will seek to live by the principles that God gives for marriage, and work hard at it, you will see harmony and wisdom and know more joy than the world can ever offer.

What I'm going to give you are some of the principles of how God created marriage so you know what God has done. The more you know of the theology behind it, the more equipped you're going to be to know how to do it well.

## Principle #1—When You Have Sex, You Just Got Hitched

God created sex to be for marriage, period. Now, a lot of Christians know that, but often times they don't know the reality behind sex. Sex is not just a physical act; it's not like a shoulder massage. There is something spiritual that happens when a man and a woman unite. In 1 Corinthians 6 the Holy Spirit speaking through the apostle Paul is warning the men not to engage in any sexual sin, and specifically in verse 16 he warns them not to sleep with a prostitute, but the reason he gives is very enlightening. He says, *"Or do you not know that the one who joins himself to a prostitute is one body with her? For He says, 'The two shall become one flesh.'"* When a man sleeps with a prostitute, he becomes one flesh with her! Where have you heard that language before? All the way back in Genesis 2:24 when Adam and Eve became the first married couple. (That verse is quoted three other times in the New Testament as well).

What that means is this, when a man and woman unite sexually, they become united in the one-flesh union that a husband and wife are. So if a young boy sleeps with his girlfriend before they are married, they are united; they are connected, and there's no undoing it. They still haven't taken vows to commit themselves to one another in marriage, but in a mystical way, they're linked together; they are glued in a way that will not come undone until death separates them. That's why people refer to having sex for the first time on their wedding night as "consummating your marriage." You marry through the vows, but you are united together in the one-flesh union when you come together sexually.

In Matthew 19, Jesus was having a conversation with some Pharisees, and here's what happened. *"Some Pharisees came to Jesus testing Him and asking, 'Is it lawful for a man to divorce his wife for any reason at all?' And He answered and said, 'Have you not read that He who created them from the beginning made them male and female'? and said, 'For this reason a man shall leave his father and mother and be joined to his wife, and the two shall become one flesh'? So they are no longer two, but one flesh. What therefore God has joined together, let no man separate."* This is why divorce is not supposed to take place. God joined you together; therefore, you don't have the right to separate. If you divorce a woman, you are trying to undo something that God has joined, so who do you think you are?

So taking all of that together, here's a conclusion. If you have sex with a woman before you marry her, you are united with her for the rest of your life. And for the rest of your life, you will take her to bed with you. If you marry another woman, every time you unite with her, there's an adulterous act happening because you are united to more than one woman. You will always be connected (so long as the two of you are alive), and it will affect your marriage. God created sex for marriage, period. Anytime that sex occurs outside of the marriage covenant it gets messy.

Do you like the thought of uniting with your wife and her bringing another man to bed with you? That's disgusting, but in a certain way, that's what happens if she unites with another man before she marries you. There's a connection that stays as long as you're alive. It's a bond that is felt. There is an attachment that remains.

The application is clear—keep yourself a virgin until you unite with your wife on your wedding night.

## Principle #2 —God Has Blessed Marriage

One of the things that you will often hear spoken at weddings, is that God created marriage. It wasn't man's idea, it was God's idea. God created it, but here's the further point that needs to be seen, not only did God create it, but He blessed it. He put His hand on marriage, He's given grace to make marriage more than just what humans could make of it. Hebrews 13:4 says, *"Marriage is to be held in honor among all, and the marriage bed is to be undefiled; for fornicators and adulterers God will judge."* The way the literal Greek reads is a little different than our English Bibles. Literally it says, "Honorable the marriage." In other words, "Marriage IS honorable." The part about letting it be *held* in honor has been added to help us, but literally what God is telling us is that marriage IS special; it IS something to be regarded with honor.

And of course there is a principle that is implied with that statement. If marriage is special, if it is sacred and honorable, then treat it that way. One cannot just treat it like common things in life. We are to regard marriage as special; it is to be that way in our minds and our hearts. If we believe that and it's impressed on us, then that will change the way we behave.

God created marriage to be a gift, and likewise the marriage bed (referring to sex) is also a gift. God wanted to give His choice creation something special. Nothing else that we know of has this gift. Animals don't, they breed and produce offspring. Angels don't have marriage, but to the creation made in God's image, He wanted to give a gift. And God blessed that gift to have powerful effects. And it does. Marriage is a source of joy, loving your spouse is a soul-enriching experience, but the warning that we are hearing is to be careful because when it is mishandled, all that power that God gave it will bring pain and chaos. Thousands of households across America can attest to that. Regard marriage and treat marriage with honor, and you will be blessed by it.

## Principle #3 —Marriage Is a Covenant

In Malachi 2:14, God addressed men in Israel and scolded them for divorcing the wives whom they were united with in a covenant. A covenant is an agreement of oaths and promises, kind of like a contract, but more than that. It's more than a technical business arrangement; it's a sacred relationship where people bind themselves with oaths.

God has made covenants with humanity. God made a covenant not to flood the earth again; God has entered in to the New Covenant with the church through the blood of Jesus. And what that means is that God has made promises to us; He has vowed to deal with us in certain ways. There is a sacred relationship.

In that same kind of way, marriage is a covenant. It's a covenant where a man and his wife make vows to each other. The vows that they pledge may vary from ceremony to ceremony and culture to culture, but there are certain aspects that are inherent, whether a person agrees with it or not. God created the covenant and the basic aspects are written on our hearts; we are all accountable. The same principles that applied at the first marriage, between Adam and Eve, still apply today.

Genesis 2:18-25 says this, *"Then the LORD God said, 'It is not good for the man to be alone; I will make a helper suitable for him.' Out of the ground the LORD God formed every beast of the field and every bird of the sky, and brought them to the man to see what he would call them; and whatever the man called a living creature, that was its name. The man gave names to all the cattle, and to the birds of the sky, and to every beast of the field, but for Adam there was not found a helper suitable for him. So the LORD God caused a deep sleep to fall upon the man, and he slept; then He took one of his ribs and closed up the flesh at that place. The LORD God fashioned into a woman the rib which He had taken from the man, and brought her to the man. The man said,*

*'This is now bone of my bones,*
*And flesh of my flesh;*
*She shall be called Woman,*
*Because she was taken out of Man.'*

*For this reason a man shall leave his father and his mother, and be joined to his wife; and they shall become one flesh. And the man and his wife were both naked and were not ashamed."*

This is the account of the first marriage covenant. Adam and Eve, before they rebelled against God's command, when they were sinless and pure, were united to each other. The essence of that covenant is the union of their lives together. There is leaving and there is cleaving. There is the leaving of one family to cleave to one's spouse and create a new family.

Marriage is a covenant where GOD, not a preacher, not the participants, not a license, GOD unites the man and his wife in a union that is lifelong. And it's a beautiful thing. Marriage is a covenant. Marriage was created by God; marriage was blessed by God; God has declared it sacred and holy, and in marriage God unites the souls of the husband and wife. Therefore …

## Principle #4 – Therefore, God Hates Divorce

Malachi 2:16, *"I hate divorce, says the Lord God of Israel."* God created marriage as honorable; He's given it as a gift. There is a one-flesh union that takes place, and it is a covenant that is intended to be for life. When a husband and wife decide to separate, they are trying to undo what God has done in the miracle of the one-flesh union, and it is breaking the vows that are made in the marriage covenant. Therefore God despises divorce.

As a young man you need to decide that this will not even be an option. You will remove the possibility of divorce from your thinking. As a man of honor, commit that you are never going to break this covenant.

## Principle #5 —Marriage Is a Lifelong Covenant

We've already made mention of the fact that marriage is intended to be for life, but there is an additional point to be made as well. Marriage is not eternal. It is life-long, but it is not eternity-long. Marriage is temporary in the scope of eternity.

Matthew 22:23-30, *"On that day some Sadducees (who say there is no resurrection) came to Jesus and questioned Him, asking, 'Teacher, Moses said, "IF A MAN DIES HAVING NO CHILDREN, HIS BROTHER AS NEXT OF KIN SHALL MARRY HIS WIFE, AND RAISE UP CHILDREN FOR HIS BROTHER." Now there were seven brothers with us; and the first married and died, and having no children left his wife to his brother; so also the second, and the third, down to the seventh. Last of all the woman died. In the resurrection, therefore, whose wife of the seven will she be? For they all had married her.' But Jesus answered and said to them, 'You are mistaken, not understanding the Scriptures nor the power of God. For in the resurrection they neither marry nor are given in marriage, but are like angels in heaven.'"*

What happens in that passage is that a group of religious leaders who did not believe in an after-life or future resurrection of any kind, were trying to trap Jesus. So they posed this scenario to Him. In the Old Testament God had given the instruction to His people, the Israelites, that if a man died without raising up a son to carry on the family name and keep the inheritance in the family, the man's brother was to marry the widow and raise up a son in the dead man's name. Thus, no family name would die out. But the Sadducees posed this scenario where a woman married seven men, all lawfully, not sinfully. Then they asked Him, "In the resurrection, whose wife will she be?" What they meant was, "In this future kingdom of heaven You keep talking about, who will be this woman's true husband, since they were all married to her?" But you see the response that Jesus gives. In the resurrection, in the future kingdom to come *they neither marry nor are given in marriage, but are like angels in heaven.* The reference to being like angels doesn't mean that we will have wings, but in the same way that angels do not marry, neither will we.

What that means is that marriage will not continue forever. Once you die, it's over. Now for some people that makes them smile; they don't want to be married to the hag they are with forever. But for others who have joyful marriages, this is a sad thought. But we have to bear this mind; we do not yet see perfectly. In the kingdom of heaven everything is going to be better. In fact Scripture says that our minds cannot comprehend what God has in store for us.

We know good pleasures here on earth, really good pleasures. Pleasures that make us long for them again. There are pleasures that are exhilarating, breath-taking experiences that happen on this earth. But the most exhilarating breath-taking experience will pale in comparison to heaven! Worship of the one true and living God, in the full light of His glory shining will be so exhilarating we couldn't handle it if we tasted it right now. All that to say, we don't understand certain aspects of what God does, but we have to trust Him that it's going to be better. One thing's for sure, we'll get along with our wife better in heaven than we ever did on earth.

## Principle #6 –Death Breaks the Marriage Covenant

1 Corinthians 7:39, *"A wife is bound as long as her husband lives; but if her husband is dead, she is free to be married to whom she wishes, only in the Lord."* When a spouse dies, the living spouse is not betraying or cheating to get remarried because the covenant has ended. That is why we often say in wedding vows, "Till death do us part."

## Principle #7 –Unfaithfulness Violates the Marriage Covenant

Mt 5:31-32, *"It was said, 'WHOEVER SENDS HIS WIFE AWAY, LET HIM GIVE HER A CERTIFICATE OF DIVORCE'; but I say to you that everyone who divorces his wife, except for the reason of unchastity, makes her commit adultery; and whoever marries a divorced woman commits adultery."* Jesus tells us there is only one reason that you may divorce a wife, if she commits adultery.

We may ask the question, "Why is this the reason?" Adultery violates the very nature of the marriage covenant, the one-flesh union. That one-flesh union is broken; now there's another person involved in that. So what God says is that if a person does this, that person's spouse is not in sin to end the marriage. It's not required to do so, in fact reconciliation would be better, but it is allowable.

There is one other time when Scripture says that you are not *bound* if a divorce takes place, and that is when a spouse insists on leaving (1 Cor 7:15). If that happens to you, and you try to fight for your marriage but she insists on leaving, then there is nothing you can do. You may bear a great deal of blame if you failed in your duties as a husband and angered her, but the act of divorce is not held against you.

## Principle #8—Marriage Is a Picture of the Gospel

God created marriage to be a gift, and when a man and his wife are living in a joyous relationship of love and harmony, that gives God glory. It gives Him pleasure, and it is also a demonstration to the world that God's ways are wise. Every time homosexual unions result in misery, it becomes evident that it is foolish. And every time marriage done God's way results in blessing and gladness, people recognize that God's wisdom is glorious, and that gives Him glory.

But there is another way that marriage gives God glory. God created marriage to be a picture of the gospel. God uses a number of living illustrations in Scripture. For instance—baptism. When a person gets baptized, his or her sins are not literally washed away by the water, and that act does not save that person. So why are we instructed to do it? One of the reasons is that it serves as an illustration. Every time we witness a new convert being baptized there is a sermon being preached without words. God has taught us the truth in Scripture that this person has died to his old life and in Christ God has raised this person up to a new life. We see the imagery of Jesus' death, burial, and resurrection.

The same with the Lord's Supper. We eat, we drink, and while we do there are truths coming home to our hearts. And the act of eating and drinking is more powerful than if a preacher just talks about the truth, the living illustration helps us comprehend the truth. Thus, God delights in it.

Marriage gives us a living illustration of the gospel. Ephesians 5:31-32 says, *"FOR THIS REASON A MAN SHALL LEAVE HIS FATHER AND MOTHER AND SHALL BE JOINED TO HIS WIFE, AND THE TWO SHALL BECOME ONE FLESH. This mystery is great; but I am speaking with reference to Christ and the church."* The Holy Spirit speaking through Paul quotes Genesis 2:24, and then he says that this is not just about husbands and wives, the bigger point is that this is about Christ and the church.

Husbands are told to love their wives *as Christ also loved the church and gave Himself up for her.* Every time a husband makes sacrifices (and that is supposed to be daily in one-hundred different ways), that's another illustration helping us to remember that Christ has sacrificed for us. Every time a husband exercises protection over his wife, we remember that Christ is now doing that with the church. Every time a wife sees the love coming to her from her husband, we are reminded that Christ loves His people.

Before I was married, I knew that God loved me. But marriage has brought the weight of that truth heavily onto my soul. There are times when I feel affection for my wife so intense it feels like my heart can't take any more. In those moments, Christ still loves His people ten-thousand times more. I understand more of the intensity of that love now that I'm living it.

God designed the entire family to be a picture of Himself. God is one God in three persons. How does that work? It's a mystery, but we at least have some help in the fact that a man and a wife are two individuals but united together to be one flesh. That helps us understand God, and that gives Him glory. God designed the family to be comprised of a father, a mother, and children. The father is called to be the leader, just as God the Father is the leader of Jesus and the Holy Spirit. Jesus gladly submits to the Father, just as the wife is called to submit to her husband. That doesn't exist in the animal kingdom, this is unique to us made in God's image. And all of this is intended to point us to Him! He is the meaning and the purpose of all things. All things exist from Him, through Him, and to Him! Every time we learn more truth about God, and every time truth becomes more real to us, we are realizing our purpose of existence—knowing and enjoying God!

When the world looks at a Christian marriage they ought to be able to see the wisdom of God, and they ought to be able to understand the truths because they see it lived out with joy. All of that will help people understand the glory of God. Marriage is bigger than just a man and his wife. We're picturing something for our children; we're picturing something for the world; we're picturing something for the angels.

Marriage, like everything else created by God, was made for His glory.

## There Is Still Hope

After reading some of these truths, you might be feeling a bit hopeless because you've already messed up.

Maybe you've already had sex, or maybe you come from a broken home, and you don't see how all of this can possibly work out right. Know this, God is bigger than any sin. The blood of Jesus is more powerful than your evil. If you've already messed up, go to God humbly, fall on your face before Him, confess it, tell Him you are sorry, and repent. To repent means to change your mind about it, to turn your back on it, and leave it. It's being sorry, but more than simply saying you are sorry, it's turning to leave it.

Scripture says that the way that we are made right with God, the way we are forgiven, the way we receive eternal life is by repenting in our hearts and looking to Christ in faith to be saved. It's not by your good deeds (you can't undo your bad ones), it's not by being good in your heart (your heart is evil), it's only because of what Christ has done in paying for sins on the cross. He lived righteously and He died to pay for sins. If you will turn to Him in faith and call out to Him to be saved, the Bible says, *"All who call on the name of the Lord will be saved."* God counts you as right with Him, all because of what Jesus has done.

If you've never really done that, I want to tell you, life has no meaning unless you belong to God. You were made FOR Him. If you ignore Him, your whole life will be a waste, and then you are going to stand before Him to be judged for your life. Every rebellious act will be judged. But God is a loving and gracious God; that's why He sent His own Son to die a gruesome death to pay for sins. And right now He will pardon you and save you from the hell you and I deserve, if you will turn to Him in faith. *Believe on the Lord Jesus Christ and you will be saved.*

If you've already turned to Him, the life of growing in Christ is a life of repenting again and again. Constantly growing, constantly seeking God, and constantly having to turn away from evil. So wherever you are, if you will turn to God, He has the power to give you joy and overcome your obstacles.

I have to be clear; if you've messed up, there are going to be consequences. Some of them will be big. But God can bless the mess and give you joy. Turn to Him, rely on Him, walk in His ways, and you'll know joy. The church is filled with people who have messed up but have experienced transformation by the gospel, and are now walking in joy. God saves, and when He does it's more than forgiving you of your past, He brings you into joy and a new life.

8

# The Call of a Husband

If you are 15 years old, you might at this point be saying, "Why in the world do I need to think about being a husband already? I'll just figure that out when I get there." That would work about as well as a quarterback walking onto the field without ever studying the playbook. If you don't know beforehand what is required of you, you are going to bomb when the time comes for you to lead. In the family you are the quarterback. You are to lead; you are to communicate the plan to the rest of the team, and then you are to execute. As a husband and a father, God has given you certain instructions for your future family. These are the plays. You need to know them before you get into the game.

## Lead

On the sixth day of creation God created man. God put Adam in the garden and entrusted it to his care. God gave this charge to humanity in general in Genesis 1:28, *"God blessed them and God said to them, 'Be fruitful and multiply, and fill the earth, and subdue it; and rule over the fish of the sea and over the birds of the sky and over every living thing that moves on the earth.'* That was spoken before the fall ever occurred, which means work was part of the original good creation, even before sin entered the world. And God specifically put Adam to work.

But very soon Adam saw that he had no helper suitable for him. So God created Eve and gave her to Adam as a helper. There's something implied in that, but then Scripture later goes on to confirm it. Eve was Adam's helper, not the other way around. Eve did not set the direction of life and lead; that was Adam's role. And the New Testament picks up on this truth and expounds it further.

It is not the wife's job to lead and set the direction for life. It's the husband's job. A man's wife is his helper—not servant, not doormat, but helper. It is the husband and father's job to set the direction for life. How will the family live? How much stuff will the family buy? What kind of standard of living will the family adhere to? How involved will they be in church life? Will the family eat together at the table or will everyone huddle around the TV? Will Christ be spoken of often with love and reverence, or will it be a topic to avoid? Will the family worship together every night? Even what kind of attitude the family adopts as its standard: will you be grateful and joyous or bitter and cold? All of that is part of the direction of life, and God calls you to lead in this. God calls you to set the tone, determine the atmosphere and the attitude, and lead the family in the way they ought to go.

Consider this, even things like using profanity in your speech typically means your wife will as well. If you watch trashy movies, your wife probably will as well. If you talk judgmentally about others, your wife will probably follow suit. That's a natural progression. But if you are careful with your speech, it's very likely your wife will follow suit as well. If you refuse to watch certain movies and state that you don't think they are appropriate, maybe your wife would just defy you and do what she wants, but most of the time (especially if you carry some weight with your leadership) she will adhere to the same standards. A great deal of weight is resting on you. Now thank God for godly women who step up to the plate and fill in when their husbands won't lead the family to Christ, but this is your job!

That's one of the primary points God makes in Ephesians 5:22-33, that passage we've looked to numerous times to see the role of a husband. We've seen that passage call husbands to love their wives; we've seen it tell husbands to provide, to cherish, and to lead, but lead to where? What is the end, the purpose, the goal of it all? Here's what verses 25-27 say, *"Husbands, love your wives, just as Christ also loved the church and gave Himself up for her, so that He might sanctify her, having cleansed her by the washing of water with the word, that He might present to Himself the church in all her glory, having no spot or wrinkle or any such thing; but that she would be holy and blameless."*

Christ loves His people with the purest love in the cosmos. Because He loves His people so deeply, He wants what is best for them. Well what is best? What would bring the greatest joy and the longest lasting joy? The kingdom of heaven and immense rewards when they get there. You are to imitate that love to your wife and children. And that is why God says that the goal of your love is to present your wife pure before God. Your job as a husband will have the same goal that Christ has with the church, to present us to God holy and blameless. Well, what does that mean? It means you are to so love her, so lead her, so speak to her, so influence her that you encourage her and support her to grow in the Lord. You are to be her pastor, her shepherd. The same way that a good pastor shepherds the flock in his care to grow in Christ and become what God calls them to be, God calls you to fulfill this role with your wife. I know you don't see that very often, I know it seems foreign, but that doesn't change the fact that your Creator commands you to do it.

## Shepherd

So practically speaking, how can a husband do this? Let's start with the most obvious. Lead your wife and family to attend a good, Bible-preaching, gospel-proclaiming, loving church that takes growing as a disciple seriously. That by itself will most often set the entire tone of the family. A good church with godly leadership will help men do this with their families. The preaching and teaching will feed your soul and your family's souls with the Word, and it will give you plenty to talk about through the week.

But additionally you need to see what Deuteronomy 6:5-9 says to dads. *"You shall love the LORD your God with all your heart and with all your soul and with all your might. These words, which I am commanding you today, shall be on your heart. You shall teach them diligently to your sons and shall talk of them when you sit in your house and when you walk by the way and when you lie down and when you rise up. You shall bind them as a sign on your hand and they shall be as frontals on your forehead. You shall write them on the doorposts of your house and on your gates."*

God commands us to live in such a way that He is on our minds continually—that literally the reason why we do everything we do is to please the Lord. We are to think of Him, not only every day, but all throughout our day. The New Testament instructs us to have a hymn of worship humming in our hearts at all times. Meaning, He is over all and in our minds continually, captivated with Him.

And specifically, fathers are given the instruction that they are to speak of the Lord to their sons and daughters every day, but not just every day—when you rise in the morning, as you're sitting at the table eating, when you are traveling, and when it's time to go to bed. That is a life that is lived walking with God. (And if it's the call for everyday living, that means it's the meaning of life).

Fathers are to do this themselves, but also lead their families to do this. Young children don't know to speak of the Lord, so their fathers start conversations about God and His Word. A father points out to his children that God is there all the time. God is God whether you think about Him or not. The oxygen you are breathing is God's; you look outside and that grass is God's, the clouds are His, the sun only shines because He upholds it; the rain that falls is because of Him. He's there and ruling whether you acknowledge Him or not.

And a temptation we face is to forget God through the week and only remember Him on Sundays. But when you speak of the Lord regularly, you're making God a part of more of your life than just a couple hours on Sunday. One part of learning to grow in the Lord is learning that He is all in all. He matters infinitely more than we give attention to Him. Scripture is continually calling us to see that everything is about God. We can go through a week and barely think of Him, but that is cosmic injustice! At all times He's worthy of worship. By speaking of the Lord you help show your children that God is a part of every moment of our lives. When you sleep He is the one who keeps the world spinning. He deserves thanks and worship for that. He provides every meal. So when you as a father speak of those things regularly and with genuine affection for Him, you're helping them see more of God's greatness and helping them love God.

You've also probably seen people who go to church and act holy but then come home two-faced. They are an angry tyrant away from the holy setting of church. What does that do for children who see that? That makes God look entirely unattractive. And it becomes obvious that his faith means nothing to him; he just acts it once a week. But now consider what it means when a man comes home from church, and for the rest of the week he speaks of the Lord, not in a condescending way, but speaks of His goodness, and they can see by the look in his eyes and the expression on his face that he means it. What does that do for his children? It makes Christ look great.

The same principles apply to husbands towards their wives. Practically speaking how can a husband lead his wife to Christ? Talk about Him. Talk about His truth. Tell your wife ways you see God's beauty each day. Tell her about questions you've had in certain passages you're reading. Ask her regularly how her Bible reading is going. Suggest to her new elements to try in her personal worship, not in a prideful way, but in a watchful and loving way. A husband who is doing his job well will be able to exhort the family to try some things. "Let's all read the New Testament over the next four months together."

In addition God instructs husbands to teach their families the Word. Husbands ought to regularly lead the family in a teaching time, maybe a ten-minute devotion in the evening before bed, or maybe something more elaborate, but regardless of the time, this is a husband and father's calling. This is not a suggestion, this is a command. I know you don't see it often, but it is COMMANDED, and men, it will be YOUR job! Not your wife's, it's your job! Take this seriously. This is your life. When you stand before God to be judged, you're going to answer for this. You, as a husband and father, aren't going to be merely accountable for yourself. As a husband and father you are also accountable for your wife and children. Just like a pastor is judged for how the flock entrusted to his care turns out, you are responsible for the spiritual condition of your wife and kids. You can't make your wife love Christ, and you can't force your kids to be saved, but you will be judged on how well you led and how diligently you sought to lead them to Christ. This is the summation of your entire life! The fruit you bear on earth will be the measure of how you are judged! And other than your own spiritual condition, your family is the highest of priorities in this life. Who gives a flip how much money you make if your kids end up in hell because you failed as a father?! This matters.

## Be

Be a godly man. You being a godly man will influence your family. When they see that you love the Lord, and you live the real deal, not acting holy but truly being like Christ, that's powerful. Godliness is powerful, and it is attractive. Godliness is having love, joy, peace, patience, kindness, goodness, and gentleness. Those attributes are beautiful; who doesn't want to be friends with that guy?

And when you treat your wife in a confident, loving, and humble way, you're going to invigorate her to want to follow you as you pursue Christ.

With your kids, God naturally wires them up to want to follow you. He gives you that help before you do anything! If you live a pure, joyful, and loving life, they are going to be drawn to Christ as they see your joy and genuineness. Proverbs says, *"Train up a child in the way he should go, Even when he is old he will not depart from it."* That is not a promise, that is a pattern. It is generally the case that great godly fathers raise up believing children. That's why a requirement for being a pastor is to have children who believe.

But if children see hypocrisy, that is a recipe for disaster. A husband and father who acts godly at church, but then comes home to act like a tyrant is going to push his family away from Christ. It happens every day. Over and over the examples pile up of men who know better, but aren't careful to follow Christ diligently, and they make their families disgusted. It leads them to believe that religion is fake; it puts a bad taste in their mouths for anything having to do with the Lord. Be godly, and you'll make Christ look great.

Leading your wife and children to Christ matters infinitely more than how much money you make. Better to live off nuts and berries from the woods and sleep on the ground than to shirk your responsibilities as a shepherd of your family! Don't let anything distract you in this. The greatest ministry you will ever have in your life is the ministry to your family. If you jack that up, it doesn't matter if you're on the cover of *Time, Rolling Stones*, and *GQ*, your life is a waste! If you mess up your family, you've lost it all. This has to matter to you.

So often, even amongst Christian men, they get so obsessed in their jobs and their hobbies that they neglect their family's spiritual life. And it's not that they don't care, but they don't get diligent to lead and do the things that lead to growth, and later in life, when their wife is barely attending church and his kids have walked away from anything to do with the Lord, he wishes he could do it all over. But it's too late. You only get one chance with your family. You only get to lead your wife once. You only get so much time to influence your kids. Make it your life's ambition to be a good family man who leads his family to Christ. You can't force them to love Christ, but you can be powerfully influential, remove all stumbling blocks, and trust that the gospel is powerful to save.

God has made you the head. That's your calling, and Satan always tempts us in the area of our calling. So Satan is going to tempt you to falter in your leadership. You will be tempted to either abuse your leadership or abdicate your leadership. Either to be too controlling and domineering, or to be too passive and never step up. Most likely, he will tempt you in both areas at different times. Watch your life, study your heart, examine your actions, and continually recommit yourself to lead in a godly way.

## Provide

The task for providing for the family falls squarely on the shoulders of the husband and father. It is one thing for a man to be injured and unable to work. In that case, a man ought to strive to find a job he can still do;, he still needs to feel that responsibility. But if he is entirely unable, then of course God does not fault him for his wife needing to work. But bear this in mind, a man sending his wife out to get a job so they can drive nice vehicles and live in a nice home and eat well while children get swept off to the babysitter, so someone else can raise them, does not sit well with the God who created mothers for the task of caring for her own children. This is a tremendous temptation that our culture is currently facing. A high standard of living has come to be expected and everyone believes they "have" to have the new car, so Mom goes to work. Mom can no longer fulfill the task that God has called her to do of caring for her children. Instead, the schools and the babysitter are raising her children.

Realize this, in that situation, money is being worshiped. It's a love of money that is driving that situation. Men—hate money! See it as dangerous. Be grieved over the greed that you see around you in culture, and vow to live differently. There are certain times in your life when you can make lots of money. Before you have kids and after they leave your home, but while you have them with you, for that short period of time, your wife has been created by God with the specific tools to care for them. Insist that she raise them, and not some babysitter you pay who will never love them like you do. If you have to work three jobs, then do it. A man sucks it up and takes care of his family. Listen closely, very closely to this verse from Scripture. 1 Timothy 5:8, *"But if anyone does not provide for his own, and especially for those of his household, he has denied the faith and is worse than an unbeliever."* Make no mistake about the job that God has called you to fulfill.

# Cherish

A marriage that honors God is a marriage where there is exhilarating love. The love God calls you to have and show to your wife is where you regard her as a treasure. *Cherish* is the word Ephesians chapter five uses.

Read these passages from Song of Solomon to see the kind of marriage that honors God. Song of Solomon 1:2-4 [The chambers were the bedroom.]; 1:12-13, 15-16 [The couch is where they made love.]; 2:2-6 [They are tasting each other, that's pretty hot!]; 4:1-7, 9-11; 5:10-16; 6:3.

This is a marriage that honors God. There is romance, there is passion, there is attraction, sex, delight, joy, and exhilaration! The husband pursues his wife because he needs her, and he delights in her, and the wife in turn delights in BEING PURSUED, and she responds to his love. His pursuit shows her he values her. When she feels valued and desirable, she blossoms. She reciprocates the passion, and the result is deep, energetic intimacy. It's good stuff!

Men, cherish your bride. Cherish her in your heart, then show her with your actions and words. Pursue her. Every couple has a different personality, but it is the general principle that, men, you are called to be the initiators of romance. You are called to treasure her. Romance is your area. Feel it in the heart. And when you do not feel it, stir it up. You have control over what you feel. Regularly bring yourself to feel affection for her, arouse a cherishing for her in your heart. Then let it ooze out. When you treasure her and pursue her, you will ignite passion in her heart and she will respond. But it starts with you. And you need to see that this takes EFFORT. **Lazy men have bad mar-**

**riages.** It takes effort to think of your wife; it takes effort to plan a gesture of affection.

Oftentimes women declare that they don't need anything huge, just a simple gesture that lets them know that they were thought of. A husband sending his wife a text message that he is thinking of her, often stirs his wife and makes her tingle. It takes 20 seconds, but the lazy husband is unwilling. There is much more to romance than an occasional text message; there are hundreds of things that could be done a day, but God's called you to pursue her.

There will be times when you don't feel like it. But honorable men keep pressing on. If you want a marriage that sizzles, you've got to initiate and work. As a man you would most likely be delighted merely in sex itself. However, your wife will need more. She has emotional needs; she has relationship needs, and conversation needs. She needs to feel cherished. She needs to know you are committed to her. She needs you to hold her and tell her everything's going to be ok. She needs you to talk to her, REALLY talk to her. She needs to feel connected to you. She needs intimacy, not merely physical, but deeper than that. She needs time. She needs attention. She needs acts of service. She needs date nights. She needs you to ask her how her day was. She needs you—to fulfill what God's called you to do. It's much easier to come home from work and plop in front of the TV and zone out, just check out of reality. But she needs you. So you muster up your remaining energy, look her in the eyes, and be with her.

Women can seem like strange creatures at times. Her needs are different than yours. You'll do some things that you think are dynamite, only to see that it means little to her. But then you'll do something simple, and it means the world. And you'll wonder why. But realize, on purpose, your wise Creator crafted her to be different. And it's a good thing. So spend your life learning how to love her. All around you, you will see lazy husbands getting by so-so, but we're not after so-so. We want what's real, what's good, REAL good. So pursue her, and pursue the calling God has put on your life.

# A Final Word

The greatest thing you can do for your church, for the kingdom, and for your family is simply to BE a godly man. The way you do that is by continually progressing. You are never going to arrive and be done. Not in this life. You will never reach a point of godliness and maturity in Christ where you can quit. The moment you quit is the moment you start sliding backwards. And it can happen rapidly! You keep pressing forward, and don't stop till the whistle blows.

Realize that the greatest ministry you will ever have in your life, is the ministry to your family. Drop the ball on them, and the rest is pretty well useless.

You've seen God's plan for your calling. Develop this mindset now. Start thinking in these terms. Start being a man of honor. Start protecting, start serving, and get serious about following Christ.

# A Word to Young Ladies

You will be treated the way you expect to be treated. Think about it, observe it around you. Notice how some girls always get treated in a certain way, no matter who they go out with or talk to. That's because they carry themselves in a way that attracts a certain kind of attention. A girl who dresses like she's for sale gets treated that way. This is why we preach hard to dads to be good to their daughters. It is generally the case, when a dad is horrible to his daughter, she grows up and marries someone like him, who is horrible to her. The cycle continues. So here's what you do. Know what honor is. Know how a man should treat a woman, then start expecting it. Start carrying yourself like you expect it. You will find that you are then treated that way. The sleeze-balls will find someone else to pursue. The great men will pursue you. You be the kind of woman that a great man would want to marry. Great men don't want easy; sleeze-balls do. Great men want great women. Be a woman that great men are drawn to. But part of that equation, is you need to know what to look for in a godly man. This book is about that.